Incredible **LEGO®** Creations

FROM SPACE

with Bricks You Already Have

25 NEW Spaceships, Rovers, Aliens and
Other Fun Projects to Expand Your LEGO® Universe

SARAH DEES

author of *Genius LEGO® Inventions with Bricks You Already Have*
and founder of *Frugal Fun for Boys and Girls*

PAGE STREET
PUBLISHING CO.

DEDICATION

**TO JORDAN AND OUR LEGO-LOVING KIDS.
CREATING THIS BOOK WITH YOU ALL WAS AN AWESOME ADVENTURE!**

Copyright © 2019 Sarah Dees

First published in 2019 by
Page Street Publishing Co.
27 Congress Street, Suite 105
Salem, MA 01970
www.pagestreetpublishing.com

Distributed by Macmillan, sales in Canada by The Canadian Manda Group.

LEGO, the Brick and Knob configurations and the Minifigure are trademarks of the LEGO Group, which does not sponsor, authorize or endorse this book.

23 22 21 20 19   1 2 3 4 5

ISBN-13: 978-1-62414-910-8
ISBN-10: 1-62414-910-3

Library of Congress Control Number: 2019940341

Cover and book design by Meg Baskis for Page Street Publishing Co.
Photography by Sarah Dees

Printed and bound in the United States of America

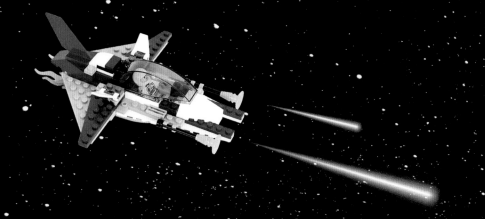

CONTENTS

HOW TO USE THIS BOOK

WELCOME, SPACE FANS!

Your mission is to create awesome spaceships, powerful rovers, alien creatures and entire space worlds!

LEGO bricks can be used to build just about anything, but of all the things to build, creating spaceships has got to be one of the BEST! It's fun to put together new spaceship designs and then to add awesome features like rocket engines and laser blasters. If you love to build space projects, this book is for you. You'll be inspired to take your space building to a whole new level!

Learn how to construct epic spaceships with room for cargo and several passengers. Follow the instructions to build a spaceship with folding wings (page 41), create alien flying saucers (page 103) and learn how to design space-training equipment. Build a powerful drill mech (page 142) and a crane rover (page 136) for space construction endeavors. The purpose of this book is to introduce you to new LEGO space projects and building techniques so that you can make amazing new projects and then go on to invent your own awesome creations!

Each of the space building ideas in this book has step-by-step instructions and a complete parts list so that you can see exactly how to assemble the project. However, don't feel limited by the instructions! Your spaceships, aliens and rover vehicles can truly be built in whichever colors you choose. If you don't have the exact bricks shown in the instructions, substitute with other colors or similar types of bricks. This is especially true for spaceships—you can put your own spin on them. You can use a different wing shape, a different cockpit or different bricks for building laser blasters. The point is to enjoy building and to create your own space worlds!

You'll also find space characters and stories woven throughout the projects that will spark your imagination to create wonderful adventures! Don't worry if you don't have the exact minifigures shown. You can use the minifigures you have to build the scenes, and you get to choose how the stories will end!

HOW TO ORDER INDIVIDUAL BRICKS

You may find that you want to build a project exactly like it's shown in this book, but you don't have all the bricks you need. It's easy to order individual LEGO bricks online.

Each LEGO brick has a very tiny ID number, usually located on the underside of the brick. These numbers can be hard to see, but once you find the ID number, it's very easy to find the brick online. Enter the ID number on Lego.com, and you'll be able to order the brick you want. Note that the ID number is specific to the brick shape only, not the color.

TIP: If you're having trouble reading the ID number on a LEGO brick, try taking a picture of the brick with a smartphone and then zooming in to see the number.

The LEGO Group has two different ways to order individual bricks. One option is to visit https://shop.lego.com/en-US/Pick-a-Brick. This is the Pick-A-Brick section of Lego.com that offers many of the most commonly requested LEGO bricks.

Other bricks are only offered through a separate area of the LEGO site called Bricks & Pieces: www.lego.com/en-us/service/replacementparts. The prices on Pick-A-Brick are a little lower, and you can order more bricks at a time. But if you're not finding what you're looking for, check Bricks & Pieces.

Another great option for ordering individual LEGO bricks is to visit www.bricklink.com. Brick Link is a site that hosts many different sellers of LEGO bricks. Think of it as hundreds of small stores inside one huge store. You can buy individual bricks—both new and used—as well as minifigures and new or retired sets. The prices on Brick Link are related to supply and demand, so you'll pay a lower price for a basic brick in a common color than you will for a rare collectible minifigure.

Keep in mind that each vendor on Brick Link charges separately for shipping, so you'll want to find one or two Brick Link stores that have all the things you need. You don't want to order seven bricks from seven different vendors and pay a separate shipping fee each time!

While you're ordering, you may want to stock up on bricks that are useful for inventing spaceships. I would recommend grabbing some extra wedge plates and both regular wedges and inverted wedges. These are very useful for creating a spaceship shape. You may also want to order some extra windshields and accessories such as tiles with computer screens and engine gauges printed on them.

LEGO bricks come in many different colors, and when you read the parts lists in this book, you may sometimes wonder which color is which! The colors are listed on the Pick-A-Brick section of LEGO.com, and the Brick Link site also has a color guide. Because Brick Link vendors sell both new and used bricks, they have a color system that includes names for older colors that have now been discontinued. The Brick Link color system is used in this book, but do note that the current light gray and dark gray bricks are actually referred to as light bluish gray and dark bluish gray on Brick Link.

Be sure to get permission from Mom or Dad before making any purchases, and get their help when using websites like Brick Link and the official LEGO site!

BRICK GUIDE

Did you know that LEGO bricks have names? You may not know any brick names because you don't need to know the names of the bricks to put together a LEGO set. The names aren't even used in the instructions. However, if you want to order extra LEGO elements online, you'll need to know either the names of the bricks or their ID numbers.

There are thousands of different LEGO elements available. This brick guide does not describe every type of brick, but it will help you understand the names and categories of the bricks you'll need for the projects in this book.

Remember, if you want to search for a brick by its ID number, you can find the tiny ID number printed on each brick, usually on the underside. Once you have the ID number, you can enter it on the Pick-A-Brick or Bricks & Pieces sections of Lego.com or on Brick Link and easily find the LEGO element you are looking for.

Please note that the names for bricks vary depending on whether you are using Lego.com or Brick Link. This book primarily uses the Brick Link system of names, although the names of some bricks have been changed or simplified for clarity. For example, you'll see bricks labeled "windscreens" on Brick Link called windshields in this book.

BRICKS

These are bricks. Count the number of studs to determine the size. For example, the yellow brick is a 2 x 8 and the red brick is a 1 x 2.

MODIFIED BRICKS

Bricks can be modified in many different ways. They may have extra studs on the side, a modified shape, such as a curved top, and added clips or pins. If a LEGO element you are looking for is brick-shaped with something extra added to it, you'll probably find it under modified bricks.

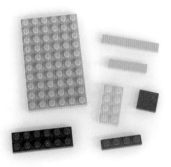

PLATES AND TILES

The flat bricks are called plates. A plate is one-third of the height of a regular brick. Plates are also referred to by size. The dark gray plate in this photo is a 2 x 6. Tiles are plates that do not have any studs on top, such as the 2 x 2 dark gray tile in the photo.

MODIFIED PLATES

As you can probably guess, modified plates are plates that have been modified in some way. They may have an added clip, handle or pinhole, for example. The dark tan plate in the photo is a 1 x 2 plate with one stud on top and is also called a jumper plate.

SLOPES

Slope bricks are so useful for building. They are referred to as "slopes" on Brick Link and "roof tiles" on Pick-A-Brick. The blue brick in the center is a 2 x 3 slope, and the light gray brick is a 2 x 2 inverted slope, meaning that it slopes in the opposite direction. The light blue brick in the front is a 1 x 3 curved slope, and the long dark gray brick is a 1 x 6 inverted curved slope. Several of those are used in this book for building the underside of spaceships.

ROUND BRICKS

These are round bricks, and they are measured in size the same way as square and rectangular bricks. The dark gray brick is a 4 x 4 round brick. The lime green brick is a 2 x 2 dome. There are also round plates that are one-third of the height of a regular brick.

CONES

Many cone bricks are used in this book! The light gray brick is a 2 x 2 truncated cone. This means that, unlike most 2 x 2 cones, it is less than two bricks high. The yellow cone in the photo is a standard 2 x 2 cone. The dark gray brick is a 4 x 4 x 2 cone.

BRACKETS

Brackets are so useful for adding pieces on the side of a creation. These are called "brackets" on Brick Link, and Pick-A-Brick refers to them as "angle plates." The light gray bracket is a 1 x 2—1 x 4, and the larger dark gray bracket is a 1 x 2—2 x 2. The smaller dark gray bracket is an inverted bracket because the second side goes up instead of down. It's called a 1 x 2—1 x 2 bracket, inverted.

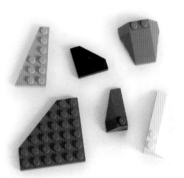

WEDGES AND WEDGE PLATES

Spaceship building requires the use of many wedge bricks and wedge plates. The blue brick at the top is a 4 x 4 wedge, triple, because it is sloped on three sides. Many wedges have either a left or right orientation. The white brick is a 6 x 2 wedge, right. To build a symmetrical ship, you'll need to have both the left and right wedges.

Wedge plates are flat wedge bricks that are one-third of the height of regular bricks. The blue plate is a 6 x 6 wedge plate with cut corners, and the light gray plate is a 3 x 6 wedge plate, left.

TECHNIC BRICKS

This book uses some Technic elements, but don't be concerned! Technic elements are widely used in lots of LEGO sets, so chances are good that you own many of them already. Technic bricks, like the dark gray brick in the photo, are bricks that have holes. Determine the size of Technic bricks by counting the studs, just as you would for regular bricks. Some Technic bricks have axle-shaped holes, such as the 1 x 2 light gray Technic brick in this photo.

Technic liftarms are smooth with no studs. You can determine their size by counting the holes. The blue liftarm is a 1 x 9. The lime green liftarm is a 1 x 11.5 double bent. This book also uses Technic axles and gears. You can determine a gear's size by counting the number of teeth, and axles are measured by how many studs long they are. The red brick is a Technic bush. These are very useful for keeping gears or other elements from sliding off an axle.

USEFUL SPACESHIP BRICKS

Here are more elements that are essential for building spaceships. The dark gray brick at the top left is called a "slope, inverted 6 x 4 double with 4 x 4 cutout" on Brick Link. You can find these under the inverted slope heading and browse for the size and color you need.

The round bricks in this photo are called dishes. The one on the left is a 6 x 6 dish, also called "radar." The smaller one to the right of it is a 3 x 3 dish. The blue brick is a 4 x 1 x 3 tail. Various windshields are also used in this book (called "windscreens" on Brick Link). If you don't have the exact one shown, you can easily substitute a different shape.

SPACESHIP DESIGN CENTER

The sun was just rising on planet Dexel. Captain Kramer looked at his intercom watch. 3:00 a.m. He sighed as he lowered the hatch on his well-worn Sky Hawk Space Cruiser. He was thinking of all he needed to accomplish before it was dark again at 10:00 a.m. Life just wasn't simple on a planet where the sun rose and set three times in each 24-hour period!

Captain Kramer started the engine and blasted off toward the Glimmer galaxy to meet up with Allie Powson. The two of them had been tasked with maintaining order between the human alliance and the pesky Cragulons, who were threatening to block all space vehicles from entering the asteroid corridor. Just then, his intercom watch buzzed. It was Allie!

"Kramer!" she said with panic in her voice. "Come quick! Cal Galvian just saw Pete's Intergalactic Transporter get struck by a huge space rock. There have been no reports of meteors in that part of the galaxy. Sounds like Cragulon work to me!"

"Ugh, I'll be right there!" Kramer said. "You help with the Transporter, and I'll get Jay to meet me at the asteroid corridor. His Z-3 Explorer can handle the challenge. . . ."

Construct a fleet of amazing spaceships using the bricks you have on hand! In this chapter, you'll learn awesome spaceship building techniques, and if you don't have the exact pieces shown, you can easily substitute other colors or shapes.

SKY HAWK SPACE CRUISER

The Sky Hawk Space Cruiser has weathered many a space battle and always comes out on top. Probably the most memorable adventure was the time that its pilot, Captain Kramer, encountered a group of Bardenoid aliens holding some Cragulons captive. Despite his annoyance with the Cragulons, Captain Kramer had to step in, and he and the Sky Hawk both ended up completely covered in slime from the Bardenoids' blasters . . . but they had won!

Build this classic space cruiser, and then give it laser blasters and flames coming from its powerful engines. Create a landing strip for Captain Kramer to use whenever he returns from his space adventures!

SPACESHIP STATISTICS

NAME: Sky Hawk

PILOT: Captain Kramer

ENGINES: Two flame-producing Infinity 7000 rocket engines

TOP SPEED: Blazes through the universe at 8,500 miles per second

SPECIAL FEATURES: Adjustable fins

HANDLING: Lightning-fast turns

SPECIAL EQUIPMENT: Two force field laser blasters

PARTS LIST

DARK BLUE BRICKS
1—3 x 8 wedge plate, right
1—3 x 8 wedge plate, left
2—1 x 4 bricks
2—1 x 2 bricks
2—1 x 6 plates
2—1 x 4 x 1 panels
1—1 x 2 tile
1—6 x 4 wedge, cutout
1—3 x 2 x 1⅓ bracket
1—tail shuttle

LIGHT GRAY BRICKS
2—8 x 8 wedge plates, cut corners
1—2 x 12 plate
2—4 x 4 plates
1—1 x 4 plate
1—1 x 2 plate
1—2 x 3 wedge plate, right

1—2 x 3 wedge plate, left
1—3 x 6 wedge plate, cut corners
1—2 x 4 brick
2—2 x 2 bricks
1—2 x 2 slope
2—1 x 2 plates with two clips on the side
2—1 x 2 grills
2—1 x 1 cones
1—6 x 2 inverted wedge, right
1—6 x 2 inverted wedge, left

WHITE BRICKS
1—6 x 4 wedge, triple inverted curved
2—4 x 4 inverted slopes, 45 degree double with two holes
1—3 x 12 wedge plate, right
1—3 x 12 wedge plate, left
1—4 x 4 wedge, triple
2—1 x 4 x 1 panels
3—2 x 2 plates
2—1 x 2 plates

1—2 x 2 curved slope
2—2 x 2 flags
2—1 x 2 plates with a pinhole on top
1—2 x 2 slope with a computer screen

ASSORTED BRICKS
1—8 x 4 x 2 windshield, curved
2—1 x 4 lime green plates
1—1 x 2 lime green plate
2—1 x 2 lime green plates with one stud on top
2—2 x 2 translucent neon yellow dishes
2—1 x 1 translucent neon yellow round plates
2—1 x 2 dark gray plates with a handle on the side, free ends
2—1 x 2 black plates with a clip on the end
2—1 x 4 black antennas
2—blue Technic pins, ½ length
2—flames

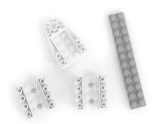

STEP 1: Gather the bricks shown for building the base of the spaceship.

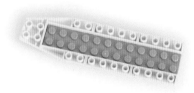

STEP 2: Use the 2 x 12 plate to join the wedges (inverted) and slope bricks.

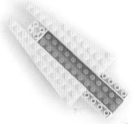

STEP 3: Add two white 3 x 12 wedge plates, one on each side.

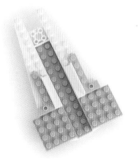

STEP 4: On each side, place a 4 x 4 light gray plate, a 1 x 4 x 1 white panel, a lime green 1 x 2 plate with one stud on top and a lime green 1 x 4 plate.

STEP 5: Grab two 1 x 6 dark blue plates, two 1 x 2 dark blue bricks, two 2 x 2 white plates, two light gray grills and a 4 x 4 wedge (triple).

STEP 6: Place a 1 x 6 dark blue plate and a 1 x 2 dark blue brick on each side of the ship. Attach a light gray grill to each lime green plate. Then stack the two 2 x 2 white plates and place them at the end of the 2 x 12 light gray plate, between the 1 x 6 dark blue plates.

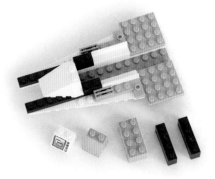

STEP 7: Place the 4 x 4 wedge on the front of the ship. Then gather the bricks shown.

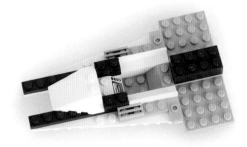

STEP 8: Attach the 2 x 4 light gray brick to the 2 x 12 light gray plate, between the 4 x 4 light gray plates at the back of the ship. Place two 1 x 4 dark blue bricks on top of it. Then add the 2 x 2 slope with a screen to the front of the cockpit and the 2 x 2 light gray slope to the back of the cockpit.

STEP 9: Grab two 8 x 8 wedge plates with cut corners and a 3 x 6 wedge plate with cut corners.

STEP 10: Use the 3 x 6 wedge plate to attach the two 8 x 8 wedge plates as shown.

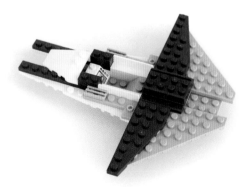

STEP 11: Attach the light gray wings to the spaceship. Then add a 1 x 4 x 1 dark blue panel and a 3 x 8 dark blue wedge plate to each wing.

STEP 12: Place a 1 x 2 white plate at the back of the ship. Then gather the bricks shown. If you don't have these exact pieces, improvise with what you have. Use regular slope bricks if you have those.

STEP 13: Attach the dark blue wedge (6 x 4 cutout) as shown.

STEP 14: Place the dark blue bracket inside the wedge cutout.

STEP 15: Attach the tail shuttle, and then place a 1 x 4 light gray plate in front of it.

STEP 16: Add a 2 x 3 light gray wedge plate to each wing. Then find two 2 x 2 white flags and two 1 x 2 dark gray plates with a handle on the side (free ends).

STEP 17: Attach the white flags to the dark gray plates and place one on each wing. Then find an 8 x 4 x 2 windshield (curved), two 1 x 2 black plates with a clip on the end, a 1 x 2 dark blue tile, a 2 x 2 white plate and a 2 x 2 white curved slope.

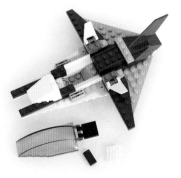

STEP 18: Connect the two 1 x 2 black plates with a clip to the windshield. Place the 2 x 2 white plate under the black plates.

STEP 19: Place the windshield on the ship. Then add the 1 x 2 dark blue tile and the 2 x 2 white curved slope.

STEP 20: Build some laser blasters for your ship! Grab two 1 x 4 black antennas. Add a light gray 1 x 1 cone, a 1 x 1 translucent neon yellow round plate and a 2 x 2 translucent neon yellow dish to each one.

STEP 21: Use a 1 x 2 light gray plate with two clips on the side to secure each laser blaster to the ship.

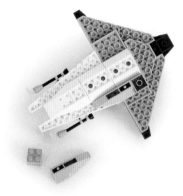

STEP 22: Turn the ship upside down. Add a 2 x 2 brick and a 6 x 2 wedge (inverted) to each side.

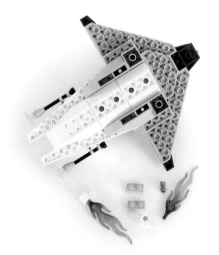

STEP 23: Insert a blue Technic pin (½ length) into a 1 x 2 plate with a pinhole on top. Then insert a flame piece. Make two of these.

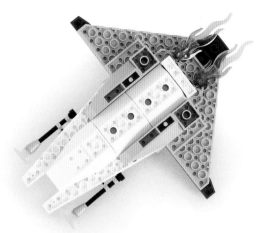

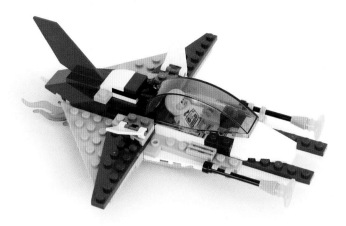

STEP 24: Stack two 1 x 2 plates (one lime green and one light gray) and attach them to the underside of the ship. Then attach the two 1 x 2 white plates with the flame pieces attached.

Now your ship is ready to fly!

Grab a baseplate and build a landing strip for your spaceship! Build a row of black plates on the sides of the runway. Use 1 x 1 round plates in translucent colors to make lights.

Set up a scene with Captain Kramer coming in for a landing after battling aliens in the asteroid corridor! Use two Technic pins (½ length with 2-stud-long bar extension) to hold lights so that one of your minifigures can direct the ship in. They might need some tools and supplies nearby so that they can get the ship ready for the next mission!

ORANGE NEBULA SPACE CRUISER

Buzz Thatcher is a space pilot with a demanding schedule. His Orange Nebula Space Cruiser is perfect for those days when there's a morning meeting of the StarCom Alliance, followed by a construction job in the new settlement on the planet Plexar in the afternoon. Once you have the spaceship's basic body shape down, you can get creative with the lasers and blasters you add to the ship. If you don't have the exact bricks shown, modify the design with the bricks you have.

SPACESHIP STATISTICS

NAME: Orange Nebula Space Cruiser

PILOT: Buzz Thatcher

ENGINES: Two Galaxy Force rocket boosters

TOP SPEED: Up to 8,000 miles per second

SPECIAL FEATURES: Titanium shell repels meteoroids and space dust

HANDLING: Nimble and quick

SPECIAL EQUIPMENT: Four hyper-focus laser blasters

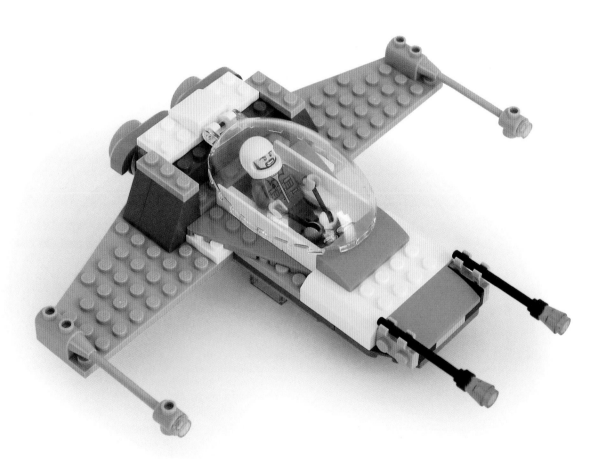

PARTS LIST

DARK GRAY BRICKS
2—4 x 8 plates
1—6 x 6 plate
1—4 x 6 plate
2—2 x 6 plates
1—4 x 6 wedge plate, cut corners
1—2 x 2 plate
2—1 x 6 bricks
1—1 x 2 brick
2—1 x 2 Technic bricks
2—2 x 2 slopes, two bricks high
2—1 x 2 slopes, two bricks high
1—1 x 2 slope with dials

LIGHT GRAY BRICKS
1—6 x 12 wedge plate, right
1—6 x 12 wedge plate, left

2—2 x 6 plates
3—2 x 2 plates
2—1 x 3 plates
2—1 x 2 plates with two clips on the side
2—wheels with pinholes
2—1 x 8 bars with 1 x 2 brick, curved top end
2—Technic pins

WHITE BRICKS
1—2 x 6 plate
2—2 x 4 plates
2—1 x 2 plates
2—1 x 4 x 1 panels
2—1 x 2 x 1 panels
1—2 x 2 curved slope
1—1 x 2 plate with two clips on the side
1—4 x 6 x ⅔ wedge, double

ORANGE BRICKS
1—3 x 6 wedge plate, right
1—3 x 6 wedge plate, left
1—2 x 4 brick
1—2 x 2 brick
2—2 x 4 curved slopes
2—6 x 4 double inverted slopes with 4 x 4 cutout
2—4 x 3 x 1 mudguards with arch, curved with cutout
2—1 x 1 translucent cones

ASSORTED BRICKS
2—1 x 2—1 x 2 black brackets, inverted
2—levers (antennas)
2—1 x 1 translucent yellow round plates
2—1 x 4 black antennas
1—8 x 6 x 2⅓ windshield bubble canopy

STEP 1: Grab two 6 x 4 orange double inverted slopes and a 4 x 8 dark gray plate.

STEP 2: Connect the two orange inverted slopes with the 4 x 8 dark gray plate.

STEP 3: Add a 4 x 6 dark gray plate and a 4 x 8 dark gray plate on top. These plates should hang off the end by 3 studs on each side.

STEP 4: Build the wings by attaching two light gray 6 x 12 wedge plates. Be sure that one is a right orientation and the other is a left. Place a 1 x 2 white plate on each wing as shown.

STEP 5: Place a 6 x 6 dark gray plate and a 4 x 6 dark gray wedge plate on the front of the spaceship.

STEP 6: Add a 2 x 6 light gray plate and a 2 x 4 white plate on each side. Then gather the bricks shown. The 4 x 6 white brick is a 4 x 6 x ⅔ wedge (double).

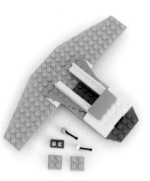

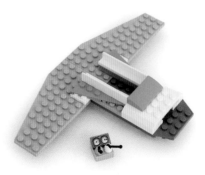

STEP 7: Place a 3 x 6 orange wedge plate on each side, and then add white panels to make the sides of the cockpit. Attach the white wedge and the 2 x 4 orange curved slope to the front of the spaceship. Then gather the bricks shown.

STEP 8: Build some cockpit controls by stacking two 2 x 2 light gray plates. Then add a 1 x 2 slope with dials and two levers (antennas).

STEP 9: Place a 2 x 2 orange brick, a 2 x 4 orange brick and a 1 x 6 dark gray brick right behind the cockpit. Then find two 1 x 3 light gray plates, two 2 x 2 dark gray slopes (two bricks high) and two 1 x 2 dark gray slopes (two bricks high).

STEP 10: Attach the dark gray slopes and the 1 x 3 light gray plates as shown to create a cool shape on the back of the spaceship.

STEP 11: Gather the bricks shown for building some engines for the back of the spaceship.

STEP 12: Add a 1 x 6 dark gray brick. Then attach two 1 x 2 dark gray Technic bricks and a 1 x 2 brick.

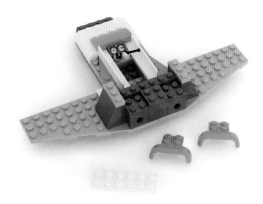

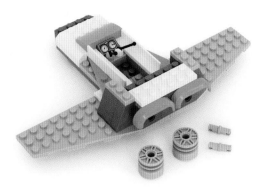

STEP 13: Attach two 2 x 6 dark gray plates and then a 2 x 2 dark gray plate on top of them.

STEP 14: Add the two orange vehicle mudguards and then the 2 x 6 white plate. Then grab two wheels and two light gray pins to make the engines. Make sure that your wheels have pinholes.

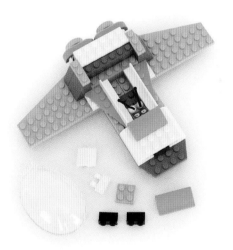

STEP 15: Insert the pins into the Technic bricks, and then attach the wheels.

STEP 16: Grab two 1 x 2—1 x 2 black brackets (inverted), a 2 x 2 light gray plate, a 2 x 4 orange curved slope, an 8 x 6 x 2⅓ windshield, a 2 x 2 white curved slope and a 1 x 2 white plate with two clips on one side.

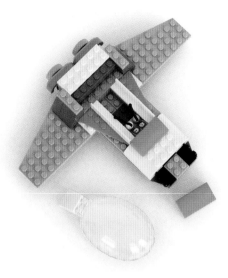

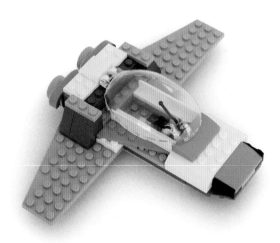

STEP 17: Attach the 1 x 2 plate with clips to the windshield. Add the 2 x 2 white curved slope. Place the two black brackets on the front of the ship with the 2 x 2 light gray plate in between them.

STEP 18: Place a 2 x 4 orange curved slope on top of the black brackets, and attach the windshield to the ship.

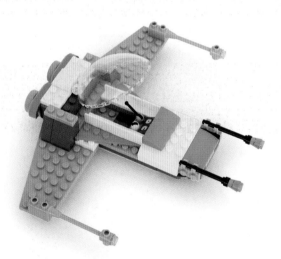

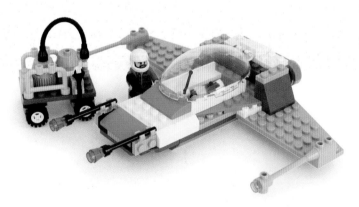

STEP 19: Now it's time to add some fun weapons. Use 1 x 2 light gray plates with clips to attach lasers made from 1 x 4 black antennas and 1 x 1 translucent orange cones. Then attach more laser blasters to the wings. The light gray pieces are called 1 x 8 bars with 1 x 2 bricks, with a curved top end. Your spaceship is complete!

Now it's time for a deep space mission! Build a small cart to hold tools and a tank for filling the Orange Nebula's fuel chamber. Once the ship is ready for space travel, send Buzz Thatcher off to another planet!

GALAXY 10 SPACE SHUTTLE

Cal Galvian gripped the controls of his Galaxy 10 Space Shuttle tightly as he navigated around a meteor that had just careened into his path. He needed to reach Plexar before negotiations between the StarCom Alliance and the Alien Council started at 6:00 p.m. He had a shuttle full of Alliance leaders who needed to be at that meeting. Suddenly, a blast of laser fire hit the side of the ship. An alien assault! Ugh! He did not have time for this!

The Galaxy 10 is an awe-inspiring space shuttle for the master builder. Equip your shuttle with powerful rocket engines, multiple sets of laser blasters, room for four minifigures and a futuristic wing design.

SPACESHIP STATISTICS

NAME: Galaxy 10 Space Shuttle

PILOT: Cal Galvian

ENGINES: Two light-year rocket engines, two turbo boosters

TOP SPEED: 4,500 miles per second

SPECIAL FEATURES: Spacious cabin, onboard communication system

HANDLING: Stable and fast acceleration

SPECIAL EQUIPMENT: Z-Tron radar communicator

PARTS LIST

LIGHT GRAY BRICKS
4—8 x 8 wedge plates, cut corners
1—3 x 6 wedge plate, cut corners
1—2 x 10 plate
1—1 x 8 plate
4—2 x 4 plates
2—1 x 2 plates
1—2 x 2 plate
2—1 x 10 bricks
1—2 x 4 brick
1—2 x 2 brick
2—1 x 4 bricks
2—1 x 6 Technic bricks
2—1 x 1 bricks
1—2 x 2 slope
1—10 x 3 wedge, right
1—10 x 3 wedge, left
1—6 x 2 inverted wedge, right
1—6 x 2 inverted wedge, left
1—2 x 3 inverted slope
1—2 x 2 round brick with ridges
2—1 x 2 plates with a handle on the end
1—1 x 2 plate with two clips on the side
2—engines, smooth with a 2 x 2 top
    plate
1—bar, 3 studs long

WHITE BRICKS
1—6 x 8 plate
1—3 x 12 wedge plate, right
1—3 x 12 wedge plate, left

1—3 x 8 wedge plate, right
1—3 x 8 wedge plate, left
4—1 x 8 plates
3—1 x 6 plates
12—1 x 4 plates
1—2 x 4 plate
2—2 x 2 corner plates
6—1 x 2 plates
1—4 x 4 plate with two clips
2—1 x 2 plates with a clip on the end
2—1 x 2 plates with a handle on the side
2—1 x 4 tiles
1—6 x 2 wedge, right
1—6 x 2 wedge, left
3—2 x 3 bricks with a curved end
4—2 x 2 x 2 slopes
2—2 x 4 slopes
4—1 x 4 x 2 panels
1—4 x 6 x ⅔ wedge, triple curved
1—6 x 4 wedge, triple inverted curved

DARK GRAY BRICKS
1—6 x 16 plate
1—6 x 6 plate
2—2 x 12 plates
1—1 x 6 plate
1—1 x 4 plate
2—1 x 2 plates
2—2 x 2 dishes
1—2 x 2 curved slope
2—4 x 4 x 2 cones with axle hole
1—6 x 6 dish (radar)
1—1 x 2 slope, 30 degree with gauges

BLUE BRICKS
4—6 x 4 double inverted slopes with
    4 x 4 cutout
1—1 x 6 double inverted slope with 1 x 4
    cutout
2—1 x 6 curved slopes
1—6 x 2 wedge, right
1—6 x 2 wedge, left
2—1 x 4 plates
2—Technic axle pins
2—1 x 4 antennas
2—1 x 1 taps (faucet pieces)

LIME GREEN BRICKS
2—4 x 4 wedge plates, cut corners
4—1 x 6 inverted curved slopes
2—2 x 2 slopes
2—1 x 1 round bricks
2—1 x 4 x 1 panels
2—1 x 2 slopes with four slots
2—1 x 1 round plates

ASSORTED BRICKS
1—8 x 6 x 2 translucent light blue
    windshield, curved
2—1 x 2 black plates with blaster
1—3 x 8 dark blue wedge plate, right
1—3 x 8 dark blue wedge plate, left
1—lever (antenna)
1—2 x 2 translucent neon green dish
2—1 x 1 translucent red round plates

STEP 1: A good spaceship needs a strong base. Start with a 6 x 16 plate, a 6 x 6 plate and a 1 x 6 plate.

STEP 2: Line up the plates, and join them with two 2 x 12 plates as shown. Then add a 1 x 4 plate.

STEP 3: Turn the base of the ship over and add a 1 x 8 light gray plate, a 1 x 4 white plate and a 4 x 4 white plate with two clips on the side.

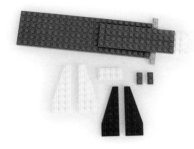

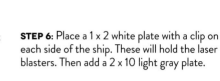

STEP 4: Flip your ship right-side up again and find the bricks shown.

STEP 5: Add a 2 x 4 white plate to the front of the ship. Then add a 1 x 2 dark gray plate on each side. Place two 3 x 8 wedge plates on each side of the ship, one white and one dark blue on each side. Substitute other colors if you need to.

STEP 6: Place a 1 x 2 white plate with a clip on each side of the ship. These will hold the laser blasters. Then add a 2 x 10 light gray plate.

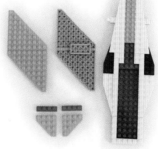

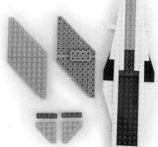

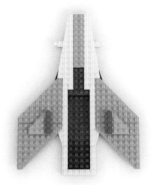

STEP 7: Place a 3 x 12 white wedge plate on each side of the light gray plate. Then add a 2 x 2 white corner plate and two 1 x 4 white plates on each side of the ship. Find two more 1 x 4 white plates and a 1 x 6 white plate.

STEP 8: Fill in the perimeter of the back of the ship with the two 1 x 4 white plates and a 1 x 6 white plate. Then build the wings as shown. Each one has two 8 x 8 light gray wedge plates with cut corners and a 2 x 4 light gray plate to hold them together.

STEP 9: Attach one wing on each side. Decorate the wings with a 4 x 4 lime green wedge plate and a 1 x 4 blue plate on each one.

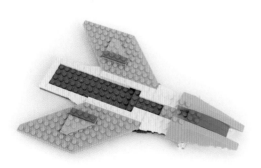

STEP 10: On the front of the ship, add two 1 x 6 blue curved slopes and two 10 x 3 light gray wedges.

STEP 11: Add a 2 x 2 light gray brick and a 2 x 4 light gray brick toward the front of the ship. Then add a 1 x 10 light gray brick on each side. Next to those, add a 6 x 2 white wedge and a 2 x 4 white slope on each side.

STEP 12: Place a 1 x 4 light gray brick in the cockpit area, and attach a 1 x 2 slope with controls printed on it as well as a lever (antenna). Then gather the bricks shown.

STEP 13: Attach a 3 x 6 light gray wedge plate in front of the cockpit controls and add a 1 x 2 light gray plate and a 2 x 4 light gray plate on each side. Then gather the bricks shown.

STEP 14: Secure the 3 x 6 wedge plate by adding the 2 x 2 dark gray curved slope. Then add a 6 x 2 blue wedge on each side.

STEP 15: Gather the bricks shown for filling in the sides of the ship.

STEP 16: Place a 2 x 2 lime green slope and two 2 x 2 x 2 white slopes on each side of the ship.

STEP 17: Attach two 1 x 8 white plates and a 1 x 4 white plate around the perimeter of the back end of the ship. Then place lime green panels on top of the white slope bricks.

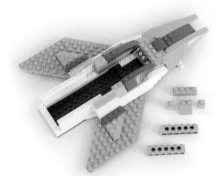

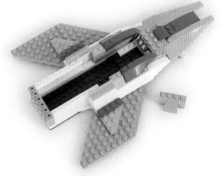

STEP 18: Fill in the sides of the back of the ship with 1 x 4 x 2 white panels. If you don't have panels, white or gray bricks will work just fine. Then find the bricks shown.

STEP 19: Place two 1 x 6 Technic bricks on the back end of the ship. Then attach a 1 x 4 brick on top of a 2 x 2 slope and two 1 x 1 bricks.

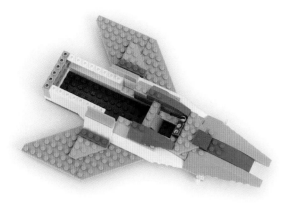

STEP 20: Place the light gray bricks that you assembled in step 19 at the back of the cockpit.

STEP 21: Grab three 2 x 3 white bricks with a curved end and attach them to the back of the ship. Then find two 1 x 8 white plates and two 1 x 2 white plates.

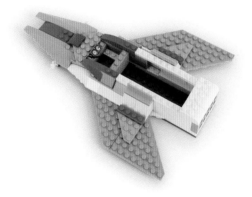

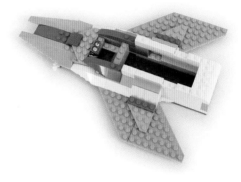

STEP 22: Attach a 1 x 8 plate and a 1 x 2 plate on each side of the ship.

STEP 23: At the back end, add a 1 x 4 plate on each side. Place a 1 x 2 plate on top of the 1 x 4 plate. Then add a 1 x 6 plate on each side in front of those. Place a 1 x 4 tile and a 1 x 2 plate on top of each 1 x 6 plate.

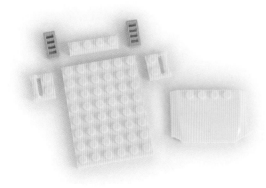

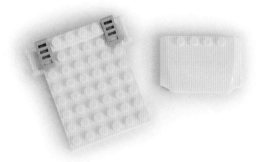

STEP 24: Gather the bricks needed for the roof. Grab a 4 x 6 x ⅔ wedge (triple curved), a 6 x 8 white plate, a 1 x 4 white plate, two 1 x 2 white plates with a handle on the side and two 1 x 2 lime green slopes with four slots.

STEP 25: Place the 1 x 4 white plate and the 1 x 2 lime green slopes on top of the 6 x 8 white plate. Then attach the 1 x 2 plates with a handle on the side to the underside of the white plate as shown.

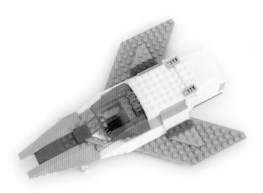

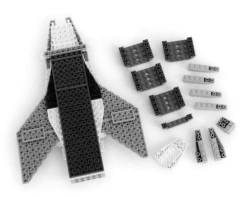

STEP 26: Attach the roof pieces to the space shuttle. The white handles will make it easy to remove the roof and to load passengers or cargo. Find a windshield. The one pictured is an 8 x 6 x 2 windshield (curved).

STEP 27: Gather the bricks shown for adding some depth to the underside of the space shuttle.

STEP 28: Place a 6 x 4 white wedge (triple inverted curved) at the front of the shuttle, and then add a row of 6 x 4 blue double inverted slopes. If you don't have enough of these, use bricks or inverted slopes.

STEP 29: Add two 1 x 6 lime green inverted curved slopes on each side of the double inverted slopes. Then place two 6 x 2 light gray wedges (inverted) and a 2 x 3 inverted slope on the back end of the ship.

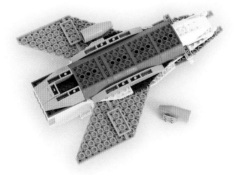

STEP 30: Add some rocket engines to each wing.

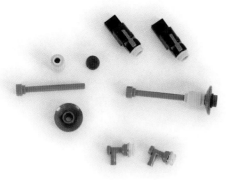

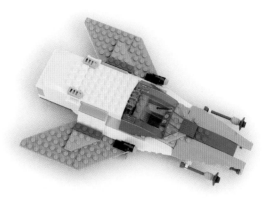

STEP 31: Now it's time to add some blasters and lights. Build laser blasters by sliding a 1 x 1 lime green round brick onto a 1 x 4 blue antenna. Add a 2 x 2 dark gray dish and a 1 x 1 translucent red round plate. Make two of these. Blue taps (faucet pieces) will make great lights! Add a 1 x 1 translucent yellow round plate to each one.

STEP 32: Use the clips on the front of the space shuttle to attach the laser blasters and lights. Attach a 1 x 2 black plate with a blaster to each wing.

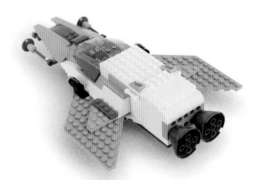

STEP 33: Add powerful rocket engines to the back of the space shuttle. Find two 4 x 4 x 2 gray cones and two blue axle pins.

STEP 34: Insert the pins into the cones and then attach them to the bottom Technic brick on the back of the shuttle.

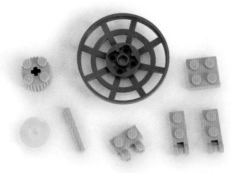

STEP 35: Build a radar mechanism for the top of the shuttle. Gather the bricks shown.

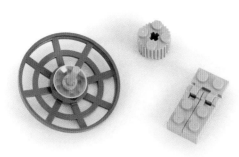

STEP 36: Place two 1 x 2 plates with a handle on the end on top of a 2 x 2 plate. Then attach a 1 x 2 plate with two clips on the side. Attach the 2 x 2 translucent neon yellow dish to the radar piece. Insert a light gray bar (3 studs long) in the center of the dish.

STEP 37: Attach a 2 x 2 round brick with ridges to the base as shown. Then attach the radar dish to the other side of the 2 x 2 round brick.

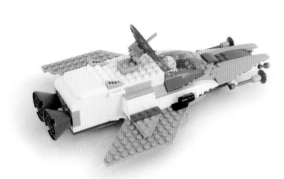

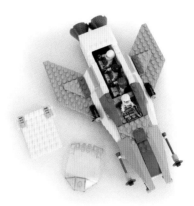

STEP 38: Place the radar on top of the ship, and the Galaxy 10 Space Shuttle is complete! Load Cal Galvian, or any other pilot, into the shuttle.

The cargo area is spacious enough for three passengers, or some cargo and equipment.

Load up your Galaxy 10 Space Shuttle with passengers, and then pretend that Cal Galvian is on a mission to transport the Alliance leaders and to help negotiate treaties to keep the universe at peace. Set up your station to blast off! Use the control center from the Rocket Launch Pad (page 82).

INTERGALACTIC TRANSPORTER

Pete Richter has been driving the Intergalactic Transporter back and forth across the Glimmer galaxy for decades. He transports scientists to the outer asteroid belt, space captains to new positions on distant planets and friendly aliens as well. There are multiple ways to configure the inside of this ship, so you can choose whether to maximize passenger space or add technical equipment.

SPACESHIP STATISTICS

NAME: Intergalactic Transporter

PILOT: Pete Richter

ENGINES: Two light-year rocket engines

TOP SPEED: 3,750 miles per second

SPECIAL FEATURES: Holds up to five passengers

HANDLING: Solid and stable

SPECIAL EQUIPMENT: Laser-deflecting Astro-Steel shell

PARTS LIST

DARK GRAY BRICKS
2—4 x 12 plates
1—6 x 6 plate
3—2 x 8 plates
1—2 x 6 plate
1—4 x 4 plate
1—1 x 8 plate
1—1 x 6 plate
3—2 x 2 plates
2—2 x 4 plates
9—1 x 2 plates
2—2 x 6 bricks
2—1 x 8 bricks
7—1 x 6 bricks
3—2 x 4 bricks
5—1 x 4 bricks
2—2 x 3 bricks
1—2 x 2 brick
3—1 x 3 bricks
8—1 x 2 bricks
1—1 x 1 brick
1—2 x 4 slope
1—2 x 2 slope
1—1 x 6 Technic brick
4—1 x 2 Technic bricks
1—1 x 8 tile
1—1 x 6 tile
1—1 x 4 tile
1—1 x 3 tile
1—1 x 1 tile

2—1 x 2 slopes, 30 degree
1—1 x 2 slope, 30 degree with gauges
1—1 x 4 brick with 4 studs on the side
2—1 x 6 inverted curved slopes
2—4 x 4 x 2 cones with axle holes
1—4 x 12 x ¾ vehicle base with a 4 x 2
   recessed center
1—2 x 2 corner brick

ORANGE BRICKS
4—1 x 6 bricks
8—1 x 4 bricks
4—2 x 3 bricks
1—2 x 2 brick
2—1 x 2 bricks
2—1 x 1 bricks
2—1 x 6 plates
1—1 x 4 plate
1—2 x 3 plate
1—2 x 2 plate
11—1 x 2 plates
3—2 x 3 slopes
1—2 x 4 curved slope
5—2 x 3 x 1 inverted slopes

LIGHT GRAY BRICKS
1—6 x 16 plate
2—6 x 6 plates
1—6 x 10 plate
1—2 x 4 plate
4—2 x 2 plates
1—6 x 4 wedge, triple inverted curved
1—2 x 4 tile

2—1 x 3 tiles
2—1 x 2 tiles
2—1 x 2 plates with a handle on the side
1—1 x 2 plate with two clips on the side
2—1 x 1 slopes, 30 degree
1—2 x 3 tile, pentagonal
2—Technic pins
1—1 x 1 tile with gauges

WHITE BRICKS
1—1 x 4 tile
1—1 x 2 plate with one stud on top
1—steering wheel
1—1 x 1 round plate with a hole
1—chair

MEDIUM AZURE BRICKS
2—1 x 1 slopes, 30 degree
1—2 x 2 plate with one stud on top
1—1 x 4 tile
2—4 x 1 x 3 tails

ASSORTED BRICKS
4—1 x 4 x 3 clear panels
4—1 x 2 x 3 clear panels
4—yellow chairs
1—2 x 4 x 2 windshield
1—2 x 4 x 2 windshield, vertical
2—tan Technic axle pins
1—lever (antenna)
1—translucent orange bar with light
cover

STEP 1: Find a 4 x 4 dark gray plate, a 6 x 10 light gray plate and a 6 x 6 light gray plate.

STEP 2: Join the plates with a 6 x 6 dark gray plate, a 2 x 8 dark gray plate and two 4 x 12 dark gray plates.

STEP 3: The underside of your two layers of plates should look like this.

STEP 4: Find a 4 x 12 x ¾ vehicle base with a 4 x 2 recessed center, two 2 x 8 dark gray plates, two 2 x 4 dark gray plates and a 2 x 4 light gray plate.

STEP 5: Attach the two 2 x 8 plates and one of the 2 x 4 plates to the vehicle base as shown.

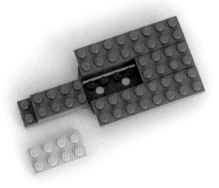

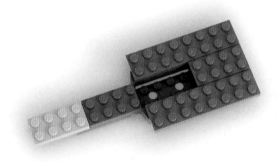

STEP 6: Attach another 2 x 4 dark gray plate under the end of the vehicle base on the other side.

STEP 7: Then add the light gray 2 x 4 plate on top.

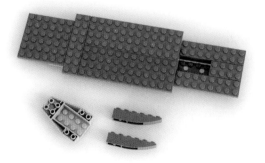

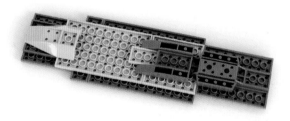

STEP 8: Attach the vehicle base assembly to the underside of the plates from steps 1 through 3. Then find a 6 x 4 wedge (triple inverted curved) and two 1 x 6 dark gray inverted curved slopes.

STEP 9: Attach the inverted wedge and the inverted slopes to the bottom of the ship.

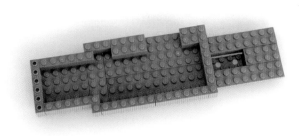

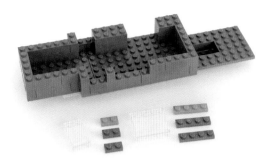

STEP 10: Turn the ship over and add a row of bricks around the perimeter as shown. The brick on the back end of the ship should be a 1 x 6 Technic brick.

STEP 11: Add a second layer of bricks to the perimeter, but leave space for windows as shown. Then find the bricks shown.

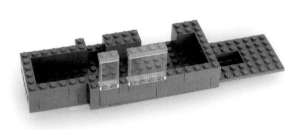

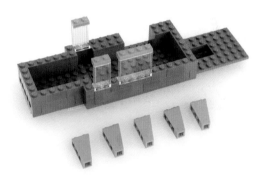

STEP 12: Place two dark gray plates in each window opening. Then add the clear panels and put an orange plate on top of each one.

STEP 13: Add a third panel following the same pattern with two gray plates underneath and an orange plate on top. Find five 2 x 3 x 1 orange inverted slopes.

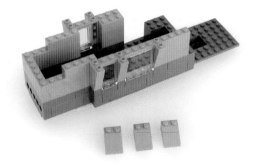

STEP 14: Place the inverted slope bricks around each window. These give the ship a really cool look, but if you don't have them, you can easily substitute regular bricks.

STEP 15: Fill in with orange bricks around the windows. Then locate three 2 x 3 orange slopes.

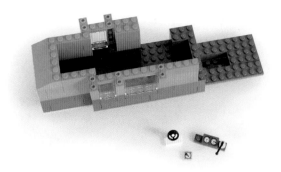

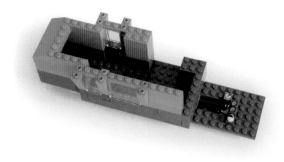

STEP 16: Add the 2 x 3 slopes to the back of the ship. Build instruments for the cockpit. Attach a 1 x 2 slope with gauges and a lever (antenna) to a 1 x 4 dark gray plate. Find a steering wheel and a 1 x 1 tile with a gauge on it. Or improvise with the bricks you have!

STEP 17: Place the steering wheel inside the recessed area of the cockpit. Then add the 1 x 4 plate and the 1 x 1 tile.

STEP 18: Stack a 2 x 4 x 2 windshield on top of a 2 x 4 x 2 windshield (vertical). Place this on the front of the cockpit, and add clear panels to make windows on the sides. Then gather the bricks shown.

STEP 19: Place a 1 x 6 dark gray brick on each side of the cockpit. Add a 2 x 3 orange brick and a 1 x 6 orange brick behind the cockpit.

STEP 20: Add a 2 x 3 plate and a 1 x 6 plate on top of the orange bricks added in the previous step.

STEP 21: Place a 2 x 2 orange brick, a 2 x 2 orange plate and two 1 x 2 orange plates next to the opening for the passenger door.

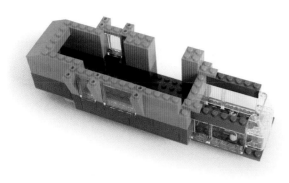

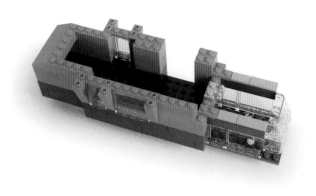

STEP 22: Attach a 1 x 6 orange plate and a 1 x 2 orange plate right behind the cockpit. Then add two 1 x 2 orange plates to connect the cockpit with the rest of the ship.

STEP 23: Add a 1 x 3 light gray tile and a 1 x 2 light gray tile on each side of the cockpit. Then place a 1 x 2 light gray plate with two clips on the side on the back of the cockpit.

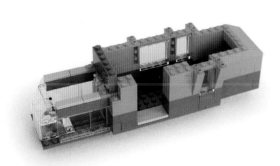

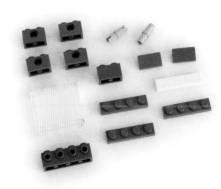

STEP 24: Turn the ship around and add a 2 x 4 light gray tile in the passenger door opening. Add two 1 x 6 dark gray bricks behind the cockpit.

STEP 25: Gather the bricks shown for building the passenger door.

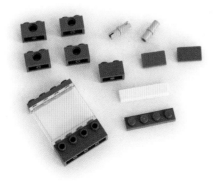

STEP 26: Attach a 1 x 4 dark gray plate to the top of the clear panel. Place the 1 x 4 brick with 4 studs on the side underneath, and then add a 1 x 4 dark gray plate under that.

STEP 27: Place a 1 x 2 dark gray brick on top of the door, with a 1 x 2 Technic brick on each side. Insert a gray pin into each Technic brick.

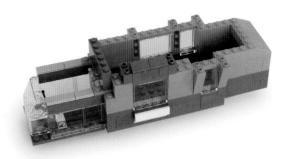

STEP 28: Use the 4 studs on the brick under the clear panel to attach a 1 x 4 dark gray plate and a 1 x 4 white tile. Then add two 1 x 2 dark gray slopes (30 degree) on top of the door.

STEP 29: Attach the door to the body of the ship.

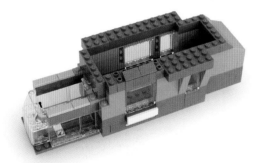

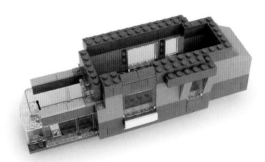

STEP 30: Add dark gray bricks around the perimeter of the ship as shown. The bricks on the back of the ship are a 2 x 2 slope and a 2 x 4 slope.

STEP 31: Now add a row of plates around the perimeter of the ship. Do not add a plate behind the cockpit.

STEP 32: Add one more 2 x 2 plate to the left of the passenger door. Add a 1 x 2 plate to the right of the door. Place a 1 x 6 plate on the back of the ship, and then on the sides. Add four 1 x 1 slopes on the front of the ship, and place a 1 x 4 medium azure tile on the side. Gather the bricks shown for the roof.

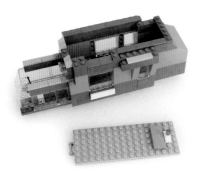

STEP 33: Attach a 1 x 2 plate with a handle on the side to the underside of the roof. If you don't have the 2 x 4 curved slope and the other bricks shown, design your own roof.

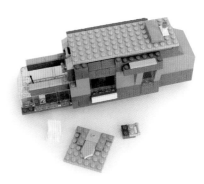

STEP 34: Place the roof on the ship. Then grab a 6 x 6 plate and decorate it to make the roof over the cockpit. Attach a 1 x 2 plate with a handle on the side and a 1 x 2 plate to a 2 x 2 plate. Find a chair to place inside the cockpit.

STEP 35: Place the chair inside the cockpit. Attach the plate with a handle to the underside of the roof. Then use the handle to attach the roof to the clips on the ship.

STEP 36: Place some 1 x 4 x 3 medium azure tails on the top of the ship for a really cool look. Add some rocket engines to the back of the ship! Insert two tan axle pins into the Technic brick on the back of the ship.

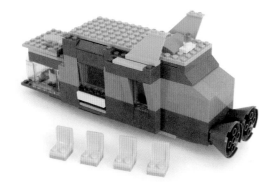

STEP 37: Attach the engines, and the transporter is complete! Now it's time to decide what goes on the inside. The transporter can easily fit four chairs. Place a 2 x 2 plate under each one.

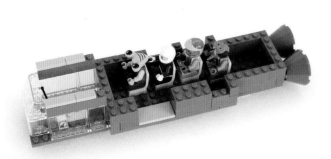

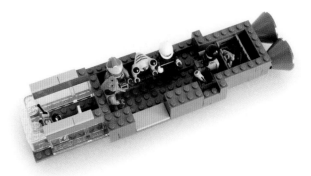

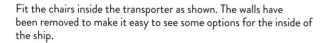

Fit the chairs inside the transporter as shown. The walls have been removed to make it easy to see some options for the inside of the ship.

Another option is to give the transporter more of a military look with a bench on one side. Use a 2 x 12 plate for the bench. Add a storage container for holding weapons.

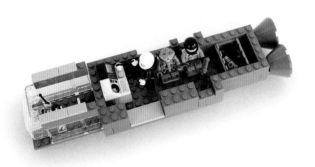

You can also add computer screens and controls inside the ship if you want to make it look more like a surveillance or research vehicle. So many awesome options!

Open the passenger door by pulling gently on the white tile.

Now your Intergalactic Transporter is ready for its first mission! Load up passengers for Pete to transport to the Research Station. Or send Allie and her Canine Cruiser to help rescue the passengers after the transporter is hit by a space rock launched by the Cragulons!

YELLOW HORNET FIGHTER SHIP

Captain Adams and his Yellow Hornet Fighter Ship are responsible for assessing the danger level of newly discovered planets so that decisions can be made about new space settlements. This makes his life quite exciting, although he sometimes finds himself in tricky situations! Thankfully his spaceship is fast and powerful. Build the ship with folding wings that can be posed in multiple positions to improve agility and handling.

SPACESHIP STATISTICS

NAME: Yellow Hornet Fighter Ship

PILOT: Captain Adams

ENGINES: Two Enron 7.5 jet engines

TOP SPEED: 7,500 miles per second in top conditions

SPECIAL FEATURES: Folding wings provide maximum agility

HANDLING: Easily darts around obstacles

SPECIAL EQUIPMENT: Variable speed battle lasers

PARTS LIST

YELLOW BRICKS
2—2 x 4 bricks
2—1 x 6 bricks
1—1 x 4 brick
1—2 x 2 brick
2—1 x 1 bricks
4—1 x 6 plates
6—1 x 4 plates
1—2 x 4 plate
2—2 x 3 plates
2—2 x 2 plates
2—1 x 3 plates
5—1 x 2 plates
1—2 x 4 brick, modified with a curved top
4—1 x 4 x 1 panels
2—1 x 1 slopes, 30 degree

1—4 x 4 wedge, taper
1—6 x 4 wedge, triple inverted curved

LIGHT GRAY BRICKS
2—6 x 6 wedge plates, cut corners
1—3 x 6 wedge plate, right
1—3 x 6 wedge plate, left
4—2 x 2 plates
1—2 x 4 wedge plate
4—1 x 2 plates with a handle on the side
2—1 x 2 plates
3—1 x 2 plates with two clips on the side
1—2 x 2 slope
2—2 x 2 truncated cones
2—1 x 4 antennas

DARK GRAY BRICKS
1—4 x 12 plate
1—2 x 12 plate

2—2 x 4 plates
1—1 x 4 brick
2—1 x 2 Technic bricks
4—1 x 2 plates with a clip on the end
6—1 x 2 grills
1—1 x 2 x 1 panel

ASSORTED BRICKS
1—2 x 2 slope with controls
1—1 x 2 hinge brick
2—1 x 1 red cones
2—1 x 1 translucent orange round plates
2—1 x 1 translucent red round plates
1—red lever (antenna)
1—8 x 4 x 2 windshield with 4 studs and a handle

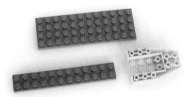

STEP 1: Build the base of your ship. Grab a 6 x 4 yellow wedge (triple inverted curved), a 4 x 12 dark gray plate and a 2 x 12 dark gray plate.

STEP 2: Use the 2 x 12 plate to join the 4 x 12 plate and the yellow wedge.

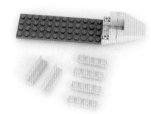

STEP 3: Add a 4 x 4 yellow wedge (taper) and two 1 x 1 yellow bricks to the front of the ship. Then gather the bricks shown.

STEP 4: Stack two 1 x 4 yellow plates on each side of the ship.

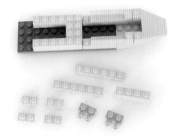

STEP 5: Then attach the two 1 x 4 x 1 panels, one on each side. Add two 1 x 6 bricks and a 2 x 2 brick to the back half of the ship. Then gather the bricks shown.

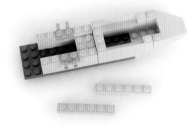

STEP 6: Place a 1 x 4 yellow brick behind the cockpit. Add two 1 x 2 yellow plates and a 1 x 2 light gray plate with two clips on the side to each side of the ship.

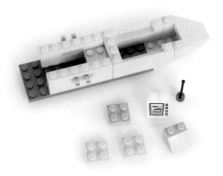

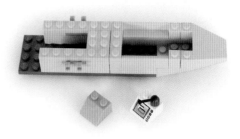

STEP 7: Attach a 1 x 6 yellow plate on each side of the ship. Then find the bricks shown for finishing up the cockpit.

STEP 8: Place the 2 x 2 light gray plate at the very front of the cockpit. Stack the two 2 x 2 yellow plates and attach them between the 1 x 6 plates added in the previous step.

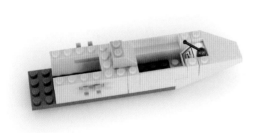

STEP 9: Use the 2 x 2 light gray slope to create the back of the cockpit. Then add a 2 x 2 slope with a screen and controls printed on it to the cockpit. Place a lever (antenna) on top.

STEP 10: Add two 2 x 4 yellow bricks to the back of the ship. Then find the bricks shown.

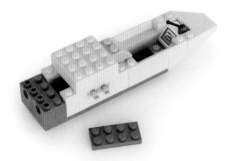

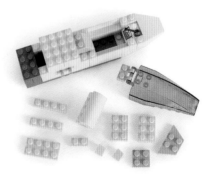

STEP 11: Attach a 2 x 4 plate to the back of the ship. Then place two 1 x 2 Technic bricks and a 1 x 4 brick on top of the plate.

STEP 12: Place the other 2 x 4 dark gray plate on top. Then gather the bricks shown. If you don't have the exact windshield shown, use what you have.

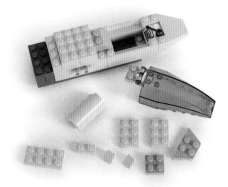

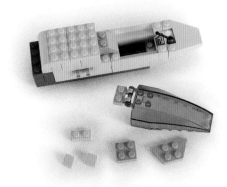

STEP 13: Stack two 1 x 4 yellow plates and attach them just behind the two yellow 2 x 4 bricks.

STEP 14: Attach the 2 x 4 yellow brick with a curved top. Then add a 2 x 4 plate on top of that. Add two 2 x 3 yellow plates.

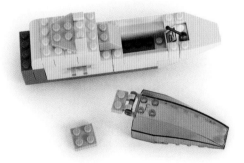

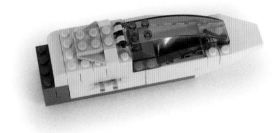

STEP 15: Use a 2 x 4 light gray wedge plate to add a fun design to the top of the ship. In front of this, add a 1 x 2 yellow plate and two 1 x 1 yellow slopes (30 degree).

STEP 16: Finish up the windshield area by adding a 2 x 2 light gray plate and then attaching the windshield in front of that. The windshield is held by a 1 x 2 plate with two clips on the side.

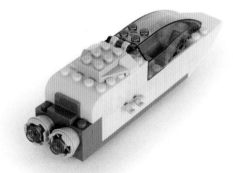

STEP 17: Find two 2 x 2 light gray truncated cones, two 1 x 1 translucent orange round plates and a 1 x 2 x 1 dark gray panel for building the engines.

STEP 18: Attach a 1 x 1 translucent orange round plate to each cone, and then use the stud on top of the cone to attach the engines to the Technic bricks on the back of the ship. Add the panel just above the engines.

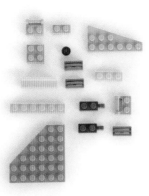

STEP 19: Gather the bricks shown. You'll need two sets of these bricks to build the wings.

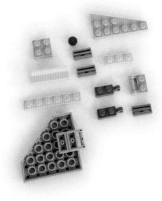

STEP 20: Attach a 1 x 2 light gray plate with a handle on the side and a 1 x 2 light gray plate to the underside of a 6 x 6 light gray wedge plate with cut corners.

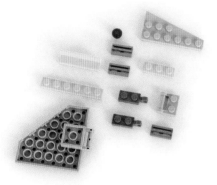

STEP 21: Secure these plates by adding a 2 x 2 light gray plate.

STEP 22: Add two 1 x 2 dark gray plates with a clip on the end. Then use the clips to hold a 1 x 2 light gray plate with a handle on the side.

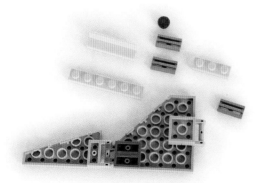

STEP 23: Attach a 3 x 6 light gray wedge plate to the 1 x 2 plate with a handle on the side.

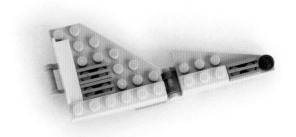

STEP 24: Turn the wings over and decorate them with yellow plates, a yellow panel and dark gray grills as shown. Add a 1 x 1 translucent red round plate to the edge of the wings. If you don't have the bricks shown, create your own wing design.

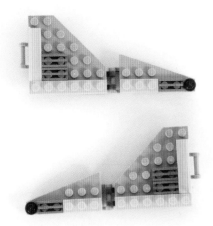

STEP 25: Build two wings that are mirror images of each other.

STEP 26: Connect the wings to the clips that are on each side of the spaceship's body. Then gather the bricks shown for building the laser blasters.

STEP 27: Insert each 1 x 4 antenna into a red cone. Attach those to the 1 x 2 hinge brick. Then attach this assembly to the roof of the ship. Your spaceship is complete!

The wings can lay flat, or you can fold up the sides. You can also fold the tip of the wings down with the center joint pointed up, as shown in the previous photo. What an impressive ship!

INCREDIBLE LEGO® CREATIONS FROM SPACE WITH BRICKS YOU ALREADY HAVE

Try building a deep space scene with a cave for Captain Adams to use as a landing spot.

Little does he know what is lurking inside that cave. . . .

Z-3 EXPLORER

As both a pilot and a spaceship engineer, Jay Zebulon designed his Z-3 Explorer with some brilliant features. This spaceship is perfect for zooming between rocky cliffs with an enemy ship right on your tail! The folding wing design allows the Z-3 Explorer to lower its wings to achieve top speeds on flat terrain and then raise its wings to navigate between rocky cliffs, and the windshield opens from the back, protecting the valuable cockpit instruments from desert sandstorms.

PARTS LIST

LIGHT GRAY BRICKS
1—6 x 6 plate
2—2 x 4 bricks
2—1 x 6 inverted curved slopes
2—2 x 2 inverted slopes
2—2 x 3 inverted slopes
1—6 x 2 inverted wedge, right
1—6 x 2 inverted wedge, left
2—2 x 2 dishes
2—1 x 1 bricks with a stud on the side (headlight)
2—1 x 1 round plates
1—flexible hose
2—vehicle exhaust pipes

DARK GRAY BRICKS
1—2 x 10 plate
1—1 x 6 brick
1—2 x 4 brick
1—1 x 6 Technic brick
3—1 x 2 Technic bricks with two holes
2—3 x 3 dishes

BLUE BRICKS
1—6 x 12 wedge plate, right
1—6 x 12 wedge plate, left
2—1 x 2 plates
1—4 x 4 x ⅔ wedge, triple curved

WHITE BRICKS
4—1 x 6 curved slopes
2—1 x 4 curved slopes
1—2 x 2 plate

2—1 x 2 plates
2—1 x 1 plates
2—1 x 1 bricks
2—1 x 1 round bricks
1—1 x 4—1 x 2 bracket
1—steering wheel

ASSORTED BRICKS
1—1 x 2 red hinge brick with a 2 x 2 hinge plate
2—1 x 2 light gray hinge bricks with 2 x 2 black hinge plates
1—4 x 4 black plate
2—1 x 1 orange cones
1—2 x 3 black tile with two clips on the end
1—7 x 4 x 2 translucent black windshield, round with handle

STEP 1: This ship is built on a small base. Find a light gray 6 x 6 plate, a black 4 x 4 plate and a white 2 x 2 plate.

STEP 2: Use the 2 x 2 white plate to connect the two larger plates.

STEP 3: Add a steering wheel and two 1 x 6 curved slopes. Then find the bricks shown.

STEP 4: Add a second 1 x 6 white curved slope on each side of the ship. Place a 1 x 1 white plate and a 1 x 2 white plate under each 1 x 4 curved slope.

STEP 5: Attach the 1 x 4 curved slopes, one on each side. Then find the bricks shown.

STEP 6: Add a 1 x 2 dark gray Technic brick with two holes behind the cockpit. Place a 1 x 2 red hinge brick (with a 2 x 2 hinge plate) on the front of the ship.

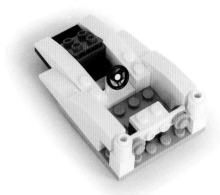

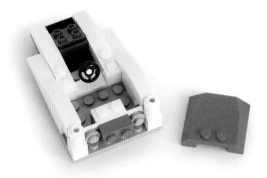

STEP 7: Place the white bracket on top of the 1 x 2 Technic brick. Then place a 1 x 1 light gray round plate on each end of it. Place a 1 x 1 white brick and a 1 x 1 white round brick on each corner of the back of the ship.

STEP 8: Attach two 1 x 2 blue plates to the white bracket.

STEP 9: Attach a 4 x 4 x ⅔ wedge (triple curved) to the back of the ship. Then find the bricks shown.

STEP 10: Turn the ship upside down and add a 1 x 6 dark gray Technic brick and a 1 x 6 dark gray brick.

STEP 11: Add a 2 x 10 dark gray plate. Then attach a 2 x 4 brick and two 1 x 2 Technic bricks with two holes on top of the 2 x 10 plate.

STEP 12: Insert a vehicle exhaust pipe into the front hole on each of the 1 x 2 Technic bricks.

STEP 13: Attach two 1 x 1 light gray bricks with a stud on the side, one in each corner of the 6 x 6 light gray plate. Then find two 2 x 2 dishes and a flexible hose.

STEP 14: Attach the dishes to the two 1 x 1 bricks with a stud on the side. Insert the flexible hose into the stud hole on each brick.

STEP 15: Turn the ship right-side up again. Find a windshield with a handle in the front, two 3 x 3 dark gray dishes, two 1 x 1 orange cones and a 2 x 3 black tile with two clips on the end. The windshield that's pictured is a 7 x 4 x 2 (round with handle).

STEP 16: Attach the 2 x 3 black tile to the red hinge brick. Then attach the windshield to the clips on the black tile.

STEP 17: Build the rocket engines by inserting a 1 x 1 orange cone into each of the stud holes in the dishes. Then attach the other side of the dishes to the 1 x 6 Technic brick on the back of the ship.

STEP 18: Construct the wings. You'll need two sets of the bricks shown.

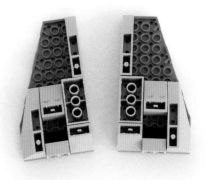

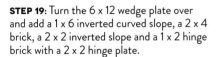

STEP 19: Turn the 6 x 12 wedge plate over and add a 1 x 6 inverted curved slope, a 2 x 4 brick, a 2 x 2 inverted slope and a 1 x 2 hinge brick with a 2 x 2 hinge plate.

STEP 20: Finish up the wing by attaching a 2 x 3 inverted slope and a 6 x 2 wedge (inverted). Then build a second wing.

STEP 21: Attach the wings by connecting the 1 x 2 hinge bricks to the dark gray plate that sticks out on each side of the ship. Your spaceship is now complete!

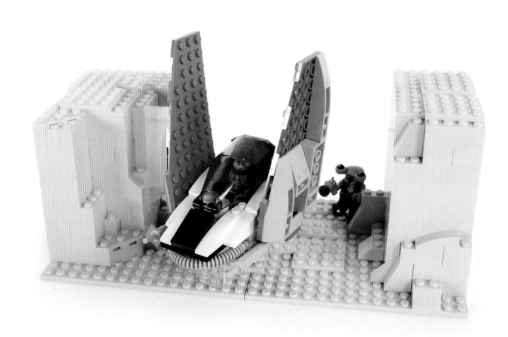

Set up some cliffs for Jay Zebulon's Z-3 Explorer to zoom through! The cliffs do not have to be solid if you don't have that many bricks. Just build walls that are one or two studs thick. Oh no, there's an alien hiding behind those rocks! And he's got a space blaster. . . . Look out, Jay!

CANINE CRUISER 4.0

Allie Powson has a unique role in the StarCom Alliance, and she loves what she does. Allie's Canine Cruiser 4.0 is equipped with double cockpits so that her doggy partner, Duke, can accompany her on missions. Between the two of them, Allie and Duke have put an end to countless enemy plots! One of their favorites was the time that they intercepted 10,000 smuggled space blasters headed for the Bardenoid aliens!

This spaceship has some awesome features. There's a storage compartment on the back of the ship. And for special missions in tight spaces, the space pods detach from the base of the ship and blast off with their own rocket engines.

SPACESHIP STATISTICS

NAME: Canine Cruiser 4.0

PILOT: Allie Powson

CO-PILOT: Duke

ENGINES: Two Infinity Force turbo engines

TOP SPEED: 7,750 miles per second

SPECIAL FEATURES: Double cockpits, meteor-resistant titanium shell

HANDLING: Powerful and stable

SPECIAL EQUIPMENT: Detachable space pods, cargo compartment

SPACESHIP DESIGN CENTER

PARTS LIST

LIGHT GRAY BRICKS
2—4 x 10 plates
1—2 x 10 plate
2—2 x 8 plates
1—3 x 12 wedge plate, right
1—3 x 12 wedge plate, left
1—4 x 6 plate
2—1 x 8 plates
6—1 x 4 plates
4—1 x 3 plates
2—1 x 2 plates
1—2 x 4 plate
2—2 x 4 tiles
2—2 x 6 bricks
5—2 x 4 bricks
3—1 x 6 bricks
4—1 x 2 bricks
1—1 x 10 Technic brick
2—2 x 2 x 2 slopes
1—2 x 2 slope
6—1 x 2 slopes
2—2 x 2 inverted slopes
4—1 x 2 x 1 panels
4—1 x 1 corner panels
4—1 x 1 slopes, 30 degree

2—1 x 4 curved slopes
4—1 x 1 round plates
2—1 x 2 plates with two clips on the side
2—wheels with axle holes
2—1 x 2 tiles with a handle
2—Technic axles, 3 studs long
1—6 x 2 inverted wedge, right
1—6 x 2 inverted wedge, left
1—2 x 2 x 2 container

DARK GRAY BRICKS
1—6 x 12 plate
6—1 x 2 plates
2—1 x 6 bricks
2—1 x 4 bricks
2—1 x 2 Technic bricks with axle holes
2—4 x 4 double inverted slopes
2—4 x 2 double inverted slopes
1—air scoop

WHITE BRICKS
2—3 x 6 wedge plates, right
2—3 x 6 wedge plates, left
1—6 x 2 wedge, right
1—6 x 2 wedge, left
2—2 x 4 wedge plates
2—2 x 2 plates
3—2 x 2 curved slopes

2—1 x 4 curved slopes
2—1 x 2 bricks, modified with a pin
2—2 x 2 inverted slopes
1—1 x 2 slope, 30 degree
1—steering wheel

DARK BLUE BRICKS
1—6 x 12 wedge plate, right
1—6 x 12 wedge plate, left
1—3 x 6 wedge plate, cut corners
4—3 x 3 wedge plates, cut corners
1—2 x 4 slope

ORANGE BRICKS
2—1 x 4 curved slopes
4—1 x 3 curved slopes
2—2 x 4 plates
1—1 x 4 brick
2—2 x 2 slopes

ASSORTED BRICKS
2—6 x 4 x 2⅓ translucent neon green windshield bubble canopies
2—1 x 1 dark red slopes, 30 degree
6—1 x 1 translucent light blue round plates
2—1 x 1 translucent red round plates

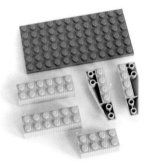

STEP 1: Grab the bricks shown for building the base of the main ship.

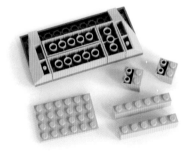

STEP 2: Attach two 2 x 6 bricks, a 2 x 4 brick and two 6 x 2 wedges (inverted) to the underside of the 6 x 12 dark gray plate.

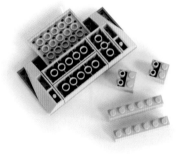

STEP 3: Place the 4 x 6 light gray plate in front of the bricks.

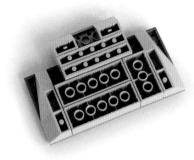

STEP 4: Attach two 1 x 6 light gray bricks and two 2 x 2 light gray inverted slopes to the underside of the 4 x 6 plate.

STEP 5: Add a 4 x 10 light gray plate. This will keep all the bricks secure.

STEP 6: Turn the base of the ship over and find the bricks shown.

STEP 7: Place the 2 x 10 light gray plate on top of the exposed light gray plate on the base. Then add one 2 x 4 light gray tile on each end and a 2 x 2 light gray slope in the middle.

STEP 8: Place two 1 x 6 dark gray bricks on the base. Then add two dark blue 6 x 12 wedge plates.

STEP 9: Turn the base 180 degrees. Add a 2 x 4 orange plate in the center. Then find a 4 x 10 light gray plate and two 1 x 2 dark gray plates.

STEP 10: Attach all three plates to the base as shown.

STEP 11: Cover the dark gray plates with two layers of light gray plates. Add two 1 x 8 light gray plates in the middle and two 1 x 3 light gray plates on each side.

STEP 12: Add a 1 x 10 light gray Technic brick. Then add a 1 x 2 light gray slope on each side. Then find the bricks shown.

STEP 13: Fill in the center of the ship with four 2 x 4 light gray bricks. Attach a 1 x 6 light gray brick to the exposed dark gray plate. Add a 1 x 2 tile with a handle to the top of each light gray slope. Then find the bricks shown.

STEP 14: Attach the 2 x 4 dark blue slope and the 2 x 4 orange plate in the center of the ship as shown.

STEP 15: Then add a 1 x 4 orange brick, two 1 x 1 dark red slopes (30 degree) and a 1 x 2 white slope (30 degree). Then place a light gray 3 x 12 wedge plate on each side. Add a 2 x 2 white plate in front of each one.

STEP 16: Add a 6 x 2 white wedge on each wing. Gather the bricks shown for building the rocket engines. The wheels will need to have axle holes. If you want to use wheels that have pinholes, substitute the Technic bricks with axle holes and the axles for 1 x 2 bricks that have a pin on the side.

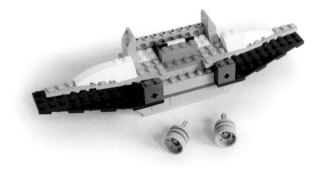

STEP 17: Attach the 1 x 2 Technic bricks (with axle holes) on each side of the ship. Stack two 1 x 2 dark gray plates on top of each one. Insert the axles (3 studs long) into the wheels.

STEP 18: Insert the axles into the Technic bricks. Then find the bricks shown. These are all used to decorate the ship. If you don't have the exact bricks shown, get creative with your own design.

STEP 19: Place a 3 x 6 white wedge plate on each side of the ship. Attach a 1 x 1 translucent red round plate to each one as shown.

STEP 20: Add the two 1 x 3 orange curved slopes and two 1 x 4 white curved slopes. Then attach two more 3 x 6 white wedge plates. These are each decorated with three 1 x 1 translucent light blue round plates.

STEP 21: Place two more 1 x 3 orange curved slopes and two 1 x 4 orange curved slopes onto the ship as shown. Then add a 2 x 2 white curved slope on each side. Gather the bricks shown for completing the main body of the ship.

STEP 22: Adding a 2 x 2 container to the ship is fun because it creates a tiny cargo area! Then add a 3 x 6 dark blue wedge plate, an air scoop, a 2 x 2 white curved slope and four 1 x 1 light gray round plates.

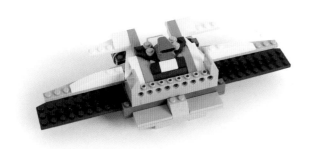

STEP 23: When you turn the ship around, it should look like this. The tile areas and the Technic brick will be used to attach the cockpit pods.

STEP 24: Build the detachable space pods. Start by attaching a 1 x 4 dark gray brick and a 2 x 2 white inverted slope to a 2 x 8 light gray plate. Then find the bricks shown.

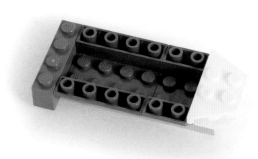

STEP 25: Fill in the center of the pod with a 4 x 4 dark gray double inverted slope and a 4 x 2 dark gray double inverted slope. Then add a 2 x 4 white wedge plate.

STEP 26: Attach a 2 x 2 slope (two bricks high) at the back of the cockpit area. Then add a 2 x 2 orange slope to the front. Find the bricks shown.

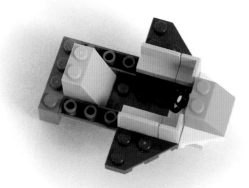

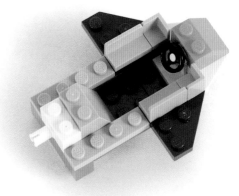

STEP 27: Build tiny wings by placing a 3 x 3 dark blue wedge plate on each side of the pod. Then add two 1 x 2 x 1 light gray panels and two 1 x 1 light gray corner panels. Attach the steering wheel.

STEP 28: Place a 1 x 4 light gray plate on each side. Then add a 1 x 2 white brick (modified with a pin) on the back.

STEP 29: Put a 1 x 2 light gray plate on top of the white brick. Then add a 1 x 2 light gray brick and a 1 x 2 light gray slope on each side.

STEP 30: Place a 1 x 4 light gray plate and two 1 x 1 light gray slopes on the back of the pod. Then find a bubble-shaped windshield, a 1 x 2 plate with two clips on the side and a 1 x 4 curved slope. The windshield pictured is a 6 x 4 x 2⅓ bubble canopy.

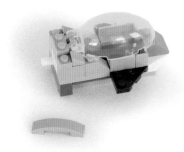

STEP 31: Use the 1 x 2 plate with two clips on the side to attach the windshield to the pod.

STEP 32: Use the 1 x 4 curved slope to secure the 1 x 2 plate with clips. Then repeat steps 24 through 31 to build a second pod.

Your spaceship is now complete!

Use the pin on the back of each pod to connect it to the main ship body.

COME ON, DUKE! WE'RE HEADED TO THE PLANET VOLTAR. I NEED YOUR HELP SNIFFING OUT SOME ROGUE ALIENS!

Load Allie Powson and Duke, or any other pilot and dog, into the ship!

Then pretend that they are blasting off on an adventure to locate enemy forces and to report back to their captain!

POCKET-SIZED MINI SHIPS

Build some astonishing spaceships on a smaller scale! These mini ships don't require a lot of bricks, and they are perfect for carrying along to a friend's house or setting up a micro scene with space mountains and alien forts. Use old bricks in new ways with this project! Brackets will allow you to use bricks as wings and small slope bricks as the cockpit on the ship.

PARTS LIST

STARCRUISER
3—1 x 1 black bricks with studs on 4 sides
2—1 x 1 black round plates
2—1 x 2 black plates with a handle on the side
4—1 x 1 dark gray round plates
1—2 x 2 dark gray dish
2—1 x 6 medium azure plates
1—1 x 4 red plate
1—1 x 4 red tile
1—1 x 1 red tile
3—1 x 2 red slopes with four slots
1—1 x 3 red curved slope
2—4 x 4 light gray wedge plates, cut corners

2—1 x 2 light gray plates with two clips on the side
2—1 x 6 light gray plates
1—1 x 1 translucent yellow plate
1—1 x 1 translucent yellow slope, 30 degree
1—1 x 1 translucent neon green round plate

GREEN FALCON
2—2 x 6 dark gray plates
2—1 x 2 dark gray slopes, 30 degree
2—1 x 1 dark gray plates with a clip, horizontal
2—1 x 2—1 x 4 light gray brackets
3—1 x 2—1 x 2 light gray brackets
1—1 x 1 light gray round brick

2—1 x 2 blue tiles
1—2 x 4 blue plate
2—1 x 2 blue curved slopes
1—2 x 2 clear curved slope with lip, no studs
2—1 x 3 x 2 lime green bricks, modified with a curved top
1—1 x 2 yellow tile with a handle
1—1 x 2 black plate with one stud on top
1—1 x 1 yellow cone
2—1 x 4 white antennas
2—1 x 1 translucent orange round plates

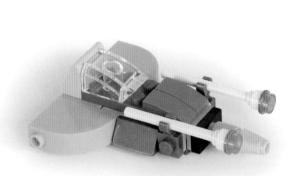

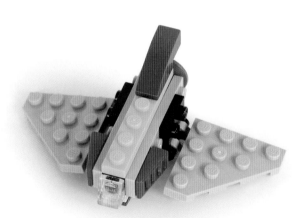

STARCRUISER

STEP 1: The red and light gray ship is constructed by attaching plates to a center core of studs. Build the pattern shown with 1 x 1 round plates and 1 x 1 black bricks that have studs on all four sides.

STEP 2: Gather the bricks shown.

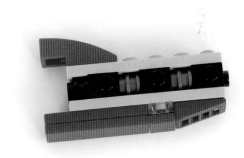

STEP 3: Attach one 1 x 6 medium azure plate to the top of the ship. Add a 1 x 3 red curved slope. Then attach a 1 x 2 red slope with four slots, a 1 x 1 translucent yellow plate and a 1 x 4 red plate to the second 1 x 6 medium azure plate.

STEP 4: Add a 1 x 4 red tile and a 1 x 1 red tile. Then attach this section to the bottom of the ship.

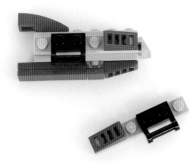

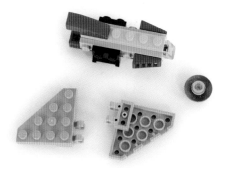

STEP 5: Place a 1 x 1 translucent yellow slope on the front of the ship. Then add a 1 x 6 light gray plate on each side. To each 1 x 6 plate, attach a 1 x 2 black plate with a handle on the side and a 1 x 2 red slope with four slots.

STEP 6: Build wings by attaching two 1 x 2 light gray plates with two clips on the side to two 4 x 4 light gray wedge plates. Attach a 1 x 1 translucent neon green round plate to a 2 x 2 dark gray dish.

STEP 7: Attach the clips on the wings to the black handles on the ship, and your spaceship is complete!

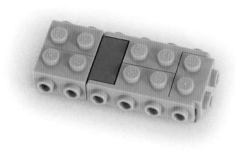

STEP 2: Attach the tile and the brackets to the 2 x 6 plates as shown.

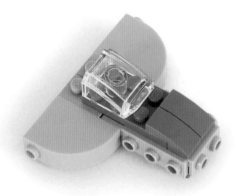

STEP 4: Add the two 1 x 2 blue curved slopes to the front of the spaceship. Then use a 2 x 2 clear curved slope (with a lip) to make a cockpit. Then attach a 1 x 3 x 2 lime green brick (modified with a curved top) to each side of the ship.

GREEN FALCON

STEP 1: Another way to build tiny ships is to use brackets to hold the wings and other parts of the ship. Stack two 2 x 6 dark gray plates, and then find the brackets shown, as well as a 1 x 2 blue tile.

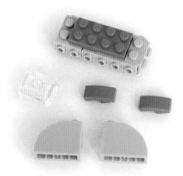

STEP 3: Place a 2 x 4 blue plate on top of the ship. Then find the bricks shown.

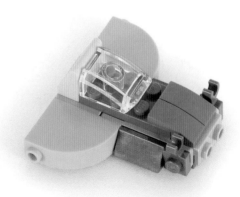

STEP 5: Place a 1 x 2 yellow tile with a handle behind the cockpit. Then add a 1 x 2 dark gray slope (30 degree) and a 1 x 1 plate with a clip to each side of the ship.

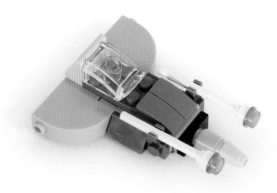

STEP 6: On the front of the ship, add a 1 x 2 black plate with one stud on top, a 1 x 1 light gray round brick and a 1 x 1 yellow cone. Then use the clips on the sides of the spaceship to hold 1 x 4 white antennas. Add a 1 x 1 translucent orange round plate to each one, and the spaceship is complete.

Now use the photos as inspiration to create more spaceship designs! There are limitless possibilities for creating tiny ships. This ship has two 2 x 4 wedge bricks on the front. The laser blasters are attached to 1 x 2 light gray plates with a handle on the side.

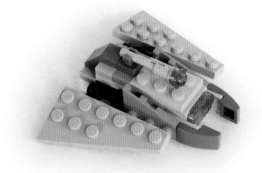

Use a bracket to attach translucent orange cones to the back to look like rocket engines.

This design is similar to the Green Falcon. Start with two 2 x 6 plates and add brackets to hold the wings.

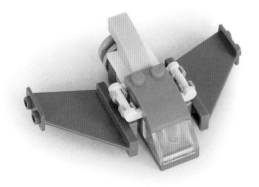

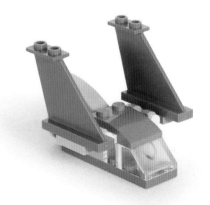

Use 1 x 2 plates with handles and with clips to make a ship with folding wings!

The wings can be folded straight up, or at an angle in between. Use a 2 x 2 clear slope for the cockpit, and choose your favorite colors for this ship.

SPACE TRAINING CAMP

Space Training Camp is where it all starts. Where the future space heroes are set apart from those who . . . well, should probably just stay firmly planted on the ground! Thankfully there are experienced leaders to see them through. Captains Jeff Allsworth and Lucy Brinker are ready to train up the new crew with the perfect combination of rigorous instruction and patient encouragement.

Create a series of stations for the new recruits to work through. They'll learn to handle challenging flight conditions in the simulator, experience G-forces in the spinning space shuttles and see what it's like to be weightless. Then send them over to the rocket station for some practice launching projectiles!

FLIGHT SIMULATOR

Time spent in the flight simulator is a crucial part of every space pilot's training. A pilot will go to flight school to learn all about flying and maneuvering a spaceship, and then the simulator provides practice in responding to any dangerous situation that might come up, such as a meteor, space dust or an alien attack. Pilots need to be prepared for anything—especially in space!

PARTS LIST

DARK GRAY BRICKS
1—2 x 8 plate
3—1 x 6 plates
1—1 x 4 plate
4—1 x 2 plates
1—4 x 4 wedge plate
1—6 x 4 wedge, triple inverted curved
2—2 x 4 inverted double slopes
1—1 x 2 Technic brick with an axle hole
1—1 x 2 slope, 30 degree
1—1 x 2 x 1⅓ Technic pin connector plate with two holes
1—1 x 2 brick

LIGHT GRAY BRICKS
1—8 x 16 plate
2—6 x 8 plates

2—1 x 3 plates
1—1 x 3 Technic liftarm with two axle holes and a pin/crank
1—1 x 2 tile with a handle
7—2 x 4 tiles
1—2 x 2 tile
2—1 x 2—2 x 2 brackets, inverted
1—Technic axle, 3 studs long
1—lever (antenna)

BLUE BRICKS
2—3 x 3 wedge plates, cut corners
1—1 x 2 slope, 30 degree
2—1 x 4 plates
2—1 x 2 plates

BLACK BRICKS
1—1 x 10 plate
1—1 x 8 plate

1—1 x 6 plate
1—1 x 4 plate
2—1 x 3 plates
1—1 x 2 plate
4—1 x 2 bricks
4—2 x 2 round plates

ASSORTED BRICKS
1—4 x 4 white wedge plate
2—1 x 3 x 2 white arches, inverted
1—1 x 2 tile with gauges
1—1 x 2 hinge brick base and 1 x 2 hinge plate

OTHER MATERIALS
Paper—cut to 3⅛ x 1⅞ inches (7.8 x 4.7 cm)
Colored pencils, crayons or markers

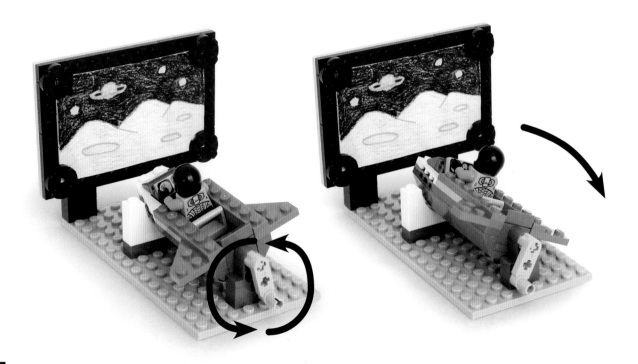

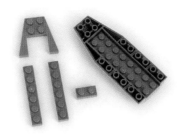

STEP 1: Grab the bricks shown to build the base of the spaceship. The curved brick for the underside of the front of the ship is a 6 x 4 wedge (triple inverted curved).

STEP 2: Use the 2 x 8 plate to connect the 6 x 4 wedge and 2 x 4 double inverted slopes to create the underside of the ship.

STEP 3: Place the 4 x 4 dark gray wedge plate on the front of the ship. Then add a 1 x 6 plate on each side and a 1 x 2 plate near the front as shown.

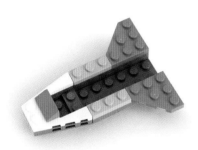

STEP 4: Give the ship some color by adding a 4 x 4 white wedge plate, a 1 x 2 blue slope (30 degree), two 1 x 3 light gray plates and two 3 x 3 blue wedge plates with cut corners. Substitute any colors you want to give the plane an awesome look!

STEP 5: Stabilize the wings by adding a 1 x 4 blue plate and a 1 x 2 blue plate on each side. Then find the bricks shown for adding controls to the cockpit.

STEP 6: Stack the two 1 x 2 plates, and place the 1 x 2 hinge brick on top. Then add a 1 x 2 tile with gauges.

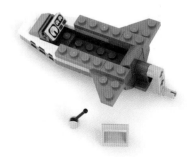

STEP 7: Place the controls inside the cockpit. Then gather the bricks shown.

STEP 8: Slide a 1 x 2 Technic brick with an axle hole, a pin connector plate with two holes and a 1 x 3 liftarm (with two axle holes and a pin/crank) onto an axle (3 studs long).

STEP 9: Attach this assembly to the back of the ship. Add a 1 x 2 dark gray slope on top of that.

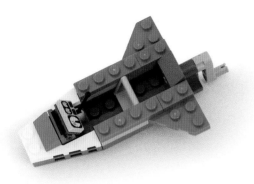

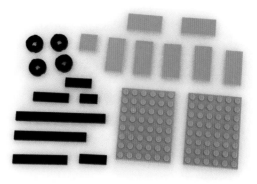

STEP 10: Place a 1 x 2 light gray tile with a handle 3 studs back from the cockpit controls. This will help define the pilot's seat. Then add a lever for the pilot to use to operate the ship.

STEP 11: Grab the bricks shown for building the screen. You can modify the design with the colors and sizes of bricks you have.

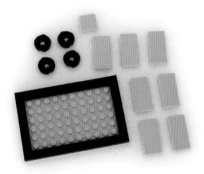

STEP 12: Use black plates to build a border around two 6 x 8 light gray plates.

STEP 13: Cut a piece of paper to fit the size of your screen. The paper shown is 3⅛ x 1⅞ inches (7.8 x 4.7 cm). Draw a space scene that your pilot will be flying through on the simulator. Make more than one option if you want!

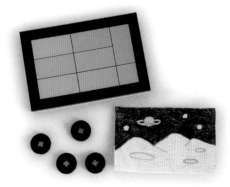

STEP 14: Attach tiles to the screen.

STEP 15: Use 2 x 2 black round plates to hold the paper in place. Put one in each corner of the screen.

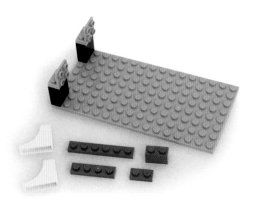

STEP 16: Build a base for the screen and the spaceship. Use an 8 x 16 plate, or connect smaller plates to create a surface this size. Then place four black 1 x 2 bricks and two light gray 1 x 2—2 x 2 brackets on one end. These will hold the screen.

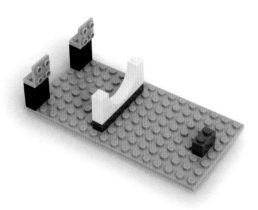

STEP 17: Place a 1 x 4 dark gray plate and a 1 x 2 dark gray plate on top of a 1 x 6 dark gray plate. Or, use two 1 x 6 plates. Place two 1 x 3 x 2 inverted arches on top of those. Then add the 1 x 2 brick as shown.

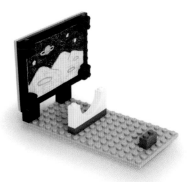

STEP 18: Attach the screen to the brackets.

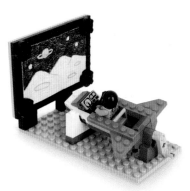

STEP 19: Rest the ship on the inverted arch bricks, and attach the end of the ship to the 1 x 2 brick. Your flight simulator is complete; now your space pilots are ready for some intense training!

If you have enough bricks, it's fun to build a second flight simulator and to set up a classroom! Build a desk for the instructors and pretend that they are coaching the students on their flight maneuvers.

GRAVITY FORCE SPINNING SPACE SHUTTLES

Future space pilots Garrett and Levi were feeling a bit overwhelmed with all they were experiencing in the intense space training program, and then their instructor led them to the Gravity Force Spinning Space Shuttles. Yikes! These did not look like an amusement park ride! Not wanting to appear like wimps in front of their instructors, they put on some brave faces. . . .

Use your fingers to spin the round bricks at the center of the machine, which will spin the shuttles around and around. The centrifuge motion will prepare your pilots for the forces they'll encounter in space travel. At the same time, your scientists can collect data on the effects of space travel on the body. Will your pilots survive?

PARTS LIST

SHIPS

The bricks in this list will build two identical ships. Feel free to swap out colors—the ships don't need to match perfectly.

LIGHT GRAY BRICKS
4—1 x 10 Technic bricks
4—6 x 6 wedge plates, cut corners
2—1 x 4 Technic bricks
2—2 x 4 wedge plates, right
2—2 x 4 wedge plates, left
2—2 x 4 plates
4—1 x 4 plates
2—2 x 2 plates
2—2 x 4 bricks
2—2 x 2 curved slopes
2—1 x 2 plates with two clips on the side

DARK GRAY BRICKS
2—4 x 8 plates

2—2 x 10 plates
2—4 x 4 plates
2—2 x 3 wedge plates, right
2—2 x 3 wedge plates, left
4—1 x 4 bricks
4—1 x 3 tiles
2—4 x 2 wedges, triple right
2—4 x 2 wedges, triple left

BASE

TAN BRICKS
2—8 x 16 plates, or one 16 x 16 plate
1—8 x 8 plate
2—2 x 2 round bricks

LIGHT GRAY BRICKS
21—2 x 4 bricks
3—1 x 8 bricks
1—1 x 10 brick
1—1 x 12 brick
4—1 x 6 bricks
1—1 x 4 brick

1—1 x 2 brick
4—1 x 16 Technic bricks

DARK GRAY BRICKS
2—2 x 4 bricks
2—4 x 4 round bricks
2—4 x 4 round plates
1—4 x 4 plate
2—2 x 4 plates

BLACK BRICKS
1—4 x 4 turntable base, free spinning

ASSORTED BRICKS
4—4 x 4 lime green wedge plates, cut corners
2—2 x 4 lime green plates
2—2 x 2 white slopes with printed computer screen
2—tan Technic pins, 3 studs long
2—8 x 4 x 2 translucent black or translucent light blue windshields with 4 studs and a handle

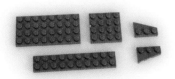

STEP 1: Build the space shuttles. Start with a 4 x 8 plate, a 2 x 10 plate, a 4 x 4 plate and two 2 x 3 wedge plates.

STEP 2: Use the 2 x 10 plate to connect the 4 x 8 plate and the 4 x 4 plate as shown.

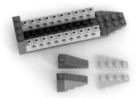

STEP 3: Attach the 2 x 3 wedge plates at the front of the ship. Then add two 1 x 4 dark gray bricks on the back. Place a 1 x 10 light gray Technic brick on each side. Then find the bricks shown.

STEP 4: Place the two 2 x 4 light gray wedge plates on the front of the ship. Then add the two dark gray 4 x 2 wedges. Then gather the bricks shown for building the wings and cockpit.

STEP 5: Place the 2 x 2 plate under the computer screen and put those in the cockpit. Then add a 1 x 4 plate on each side. Build the wings using the wedge plates with cut corners.

STEP 6: Add a 1 x 4 light gray Technic brick and a 2 x 4 light gray brick on the back of the shuttle. Then gather the bricks shown.

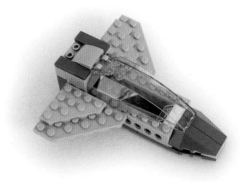

STEP 7: Place a 2 x 4 light gray plate and a 2 x 4 lime green plate on top of the 2 x 4 brick. Then add the 1 x 2 plate with two clips on the side and an 8 x 4 x 2 windshield.

STEP 8: Cover the 1 x 2 plate with clips with a 2 x 2 curved slope. Add a 1 x 3 dark gray tile on each side for extra support. Then repeat steps 1 through 8 to build a second space shuttle. If you want, feel free to use a different color for the wedge plates on the wings and change the color of the wedge on the nose of the ship.

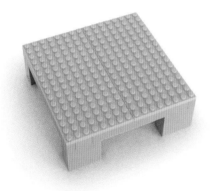

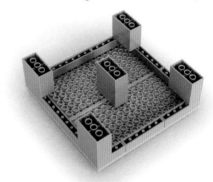

STEP 9: Construct a base for your spinning space shuttles. Use two 8 x 16 plates or one 16 x 16 plate.

STEP 10: Support the base by building a row of bricks around the perimeter. Then add four 2 x 4 bricks in the center and three 2 x 4 bricks on each corner.

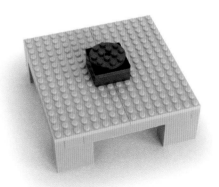

STEP 11: Put two 2 x 4 dark gray bricks in the center of your base. Then find a 4 x 4 turntable base, a 4 x 4 dark gray round plate and a 4 x 4 dark gray plate. The turntable base should be the kind that allows a round plate attached to it to spin freely.

STEP 12: Place the 4 x 4 plate on top of the dark gray bricks. Then stack the turntable base and the 4 x 4 round plate on top.

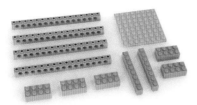

STEP 13: Gather the bricks shown for building the spinning arms of the machine.

STEP 14: Attach the light gray bricks and the 1 x 16 Technic bricks to the 8 x 8 plate as shown.

STEP 15: Attach a 6 x 6 dark gray plate in the center of the arms assembly. Then add two 2 x 2 tan round bricks. Place a 2 x 4 plate at the end of each arm for stability. Add two 4 x 4 dark gray round bricks and one 4 x 4 dark gray round plate to the center of the base.

STEP 16: Add the arms assembly to the base by attaching it to the round bricks. Then grab your space shuttles and two pins (3 studs long). The pins should not have friction ridges because they need to allow the shuttles to rotate freely.

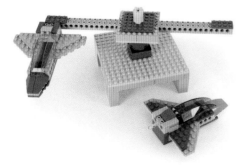

STEP 17: Slide the pins through both Technic bricks on each arm, and then through the back of each shuttle.

Once you've attached both space shuttles, your machine is complete! Try giving the shuttles a spin!

OKAY, IT'S TIME TO BOARD YOUR SPACESHIPS!

Now set up a scene with researchers and two pilots who are getting ready for training. Add steps made from 2 x 4 bricks that lead up to the base.

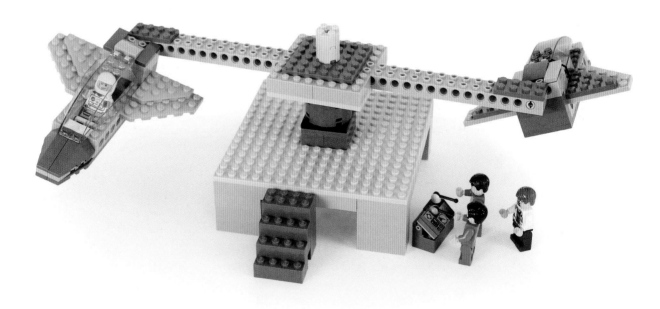

As the ships spin, they will tilt outward from the force of the spinning. Test your machine and see if the speed of the spinning affects how much the ships tilt!

WEIGHTLESSNESS TRAINING

This crazy contraption simulates the disorientation that a person can feel in space due to weightlessness. When you're floating around inside a space shuttle, it's hard to tell which way is up! Like the real multi-axis trainer used by NASA, this machine turns LEGO minifigures upside-down and around, rotating on more than one axis at a time.

PARTS LIST

DARK TAN BRICKS
2—16 x 16 plates
1—6 x 12 plate
2—Technic axles, 5 studs long with stop

LIGHT GRAY BRICKS
1—Technic gear, 40 tooth
2—1 x 9 Technic liftarms
1—1 x 7 Technic liftarm
1—1 x 12 Technic brick
1—1 x 6 Technic brick
4—Technic axle and pin connectors, perpendicular, 3 studs long with a center pinhole
2—Technic axle and pin connectors, 3 studs long with two pinholes

2—1 x 3 Technic liftarms with two axle holes and pin/crank
2—Technic axles, 7 studs long
5—Technic axles, 5 studs long
8—Technic axles, 3 studs long
1—Technic bush

DARK GRAY BRICKS
2—1 x 14 Technic bricks
2—1 x 11 Technic liftarms
2—3 x 3 Technic liftarms, T-shaped thick
1—Technic gear, 8 tooth
1—Technic gear, 24 tooth
2—Technic axles, 4 studs long with stop

YELLOW BRICKS
4—1 x 5 Technic liftarms
6—1 x 11.5 Technic liftarms, double bent
2—Technic bushes, ½ length

ASSORTED BRICKS
1—red Technic axle, 2 studs long notched
5—red Technic connectors, 2 studs long
4—red Technic pins, 3 studs long with bush
2—red Technic bushes
15—black Technic pins with friction ridges
2—black Technic axle and pin connectors, perpendicular
3—blue Technic axle pins with friction ridges
1—tan Technic axle pin without friction ridges
1—black Technic bevel gear, 20 tooth
1—tan Technic half bevel gear, 12 tooth
1—blue chair

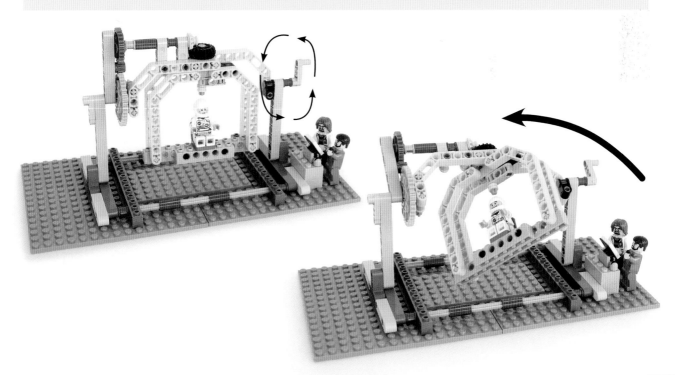

STEP 1: Build a base for your weightlessness training machine by connecting two 16 x 16 plates with a 6 x 12 plate.

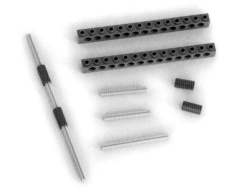

STEP 2: Use two Technic connectors to attach two axles (5 studs long) and one axle (7 studs long). Build two of these. Find two 1 x 14 Technic bricks.

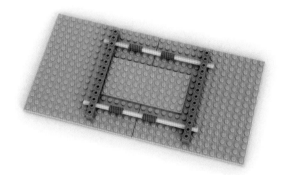

STEP 3: Place the two 1 x 14 Technic bricks on the base with the axles running through the second-to-last hole in each one. There should be 13 studs between the Technic bricks.

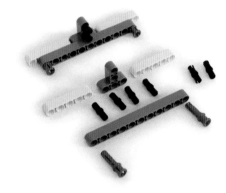

STEP 4: Find four 1 x 5 yellow liftarms and two 1 x 11 dark gray liftarms. You'll also need two 3 x 3 dark gray T-shaped liftarms, twelve black pins with friction ridges and four red pins (3 studs long with bush). Use the pins to connect the liftarms as shown.

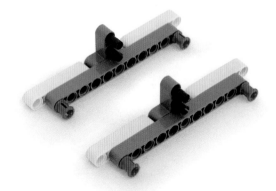

STEP 5: Build two identical liftarm assemblies.

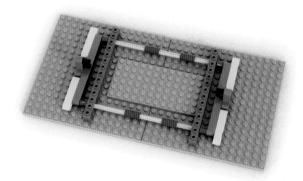

STEP 6: Slide the liftarm assemblies onto the axles. The axles will fit inside the red Technic bushes on each side of the liftarm assembly.

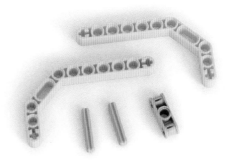

STEP 7: Add a 1 x 9 light gray liftarm on each side by sliding it onto the black pins.

STEP 8: Find two 1 x 11.5 yellow liftarms (double bent), an axle and pin connector (perpendicular, 3 studs long with a center pinhole) and two axles (3 studs long).

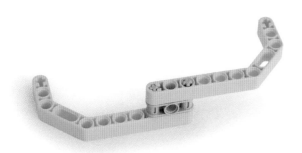

STEP 9: Use the axles to attach the liftarms as shown.

STEP 10: Begin building the mechanism. Use two more axles (3 studs long) to attach another axle and pin connector (perpendicular, 3 studs long with a center pinhole). Then find a blue axle pin, a black axle and pin connector (perpendicular), a 20-tooth Technic bevel gear and an axle (5 studs long with a stop).

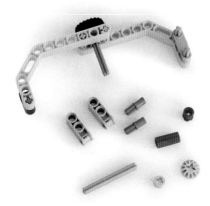

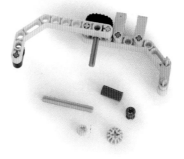

STEP 11: Slide the axle (5 studs long with a stop) through the 20-tooth bevel gear, and insert this in the top of the frame. Then use the blue axle pin to attach the black axle and pin connector (perpendicular) to the side of the frame. Gather the bricks shown.

STEP 12: Use two blue axle pins to attach two axle and pin connectors (3 studs long with two pinholes) to the frame as shown.

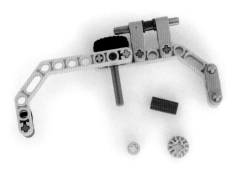

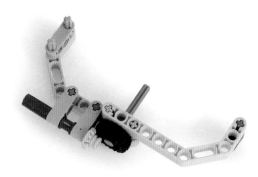

STEP 13: Slide an axle (5 studs long) and a red Technic bush through the axle and pin connectors that you added in step 12.

STEP 14: Slide a red connector onto the exposed axle on the outside of the frame. Add a tan 12-tooth half bevel gear on the axle on the other side so that it meshes with the 20-tooth bevel gear. Secure it with a yellow bush (½ length).

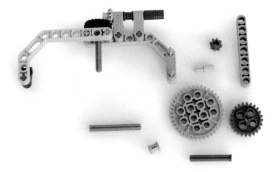

STEP 15: Gather the pieces shown. You'll need a 40-tooth gear, a 24-tooth gear, an 8-tooth gear, a tan axle pin (no friction ridges), a dark tan axle (5 studs long with a stop), a dark gray axle (4 studs long with a stop), a light gray bush and a 1 x 7 light gray liftarm.

STEP 16: Use the dark tan axle (5 studs long with a stop) to attach the 40-tooth gear to the frame. Slide the axle through the center pinhole in the axle and pin connector and then through the gear.

STEP 17: Slide the dark gray axle (4 studs long with a stop) and the tan axle pin into the second and fourth holes in the liftarm.

STEP 18: Slide the 24-tooth gear and the light gray bush onto the axle. Slide the 8-tooth gear onto the axle pin.

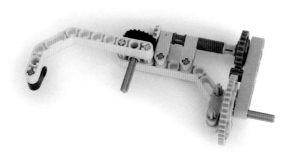

STEP 19: Slide the liftarm onto the dark tan axle that you added in step 16. Slide the axle into the red connector at the top of the frame.

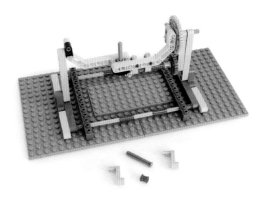

STEP 20: Add the mechanism to the main frame by sliding the dark tan axle into the liftarm on the right. The left side is not yet attached. Find a dark gray axle (4 studs long with a stop), a red Technic bush and two 1 x 3 liftarms (with two axle holes and a pin/crank).

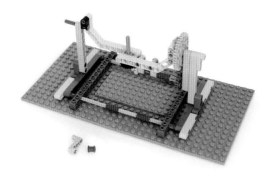

STEP 21: Attach one of the 1 x 3 liftarms on the right side. Slide the axle (4 studs long with a stop) through the black axle and pin connector and the light gray liftarm on the left side.

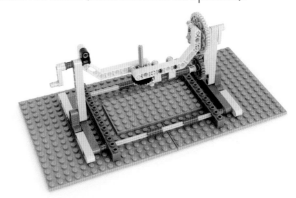

STEP 22: Slide the red Technic bush and the other 1 x 3 liftarm onto the axle. Now you have a crank for turning the mechanism.

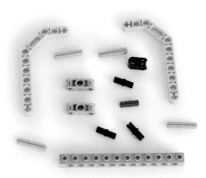

STEP 23: Gather the bricks shown for building the chair that the astronaut will sit in.

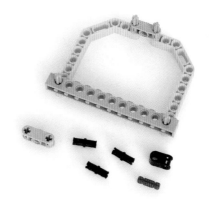

STEP 24: Use two axles (3 studs long) to attach a 1 x 12 Technic brick to the bottom of two 1 x 11.5 liftarms (double bent). Use two more axles (3 studs long) to connect the tops of the liftarms with an axle and pin connector (3 studs long with a center pinhole).

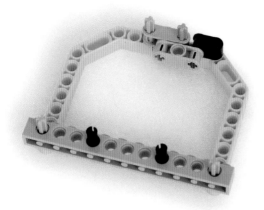

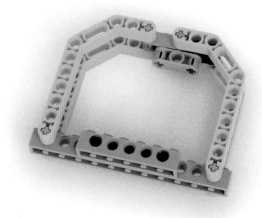

STEP 25: Insert two black pins into the Technic brick. Each should be on the fourth hole from the end. Connect a black axle and pin connector (perpendicular) and a light gray axle and pin connector (3 studs long with a center pinhole) using a red axle (2 studs long). Then attach these to the frame by inserting a black pin into the black axle and pin connector and into the frame.

STEP 26: Slide two more 1 x 11.5 liftarms (double bent) onto the axles. Use the black pins to attach a 1 x 6 Technic brick.

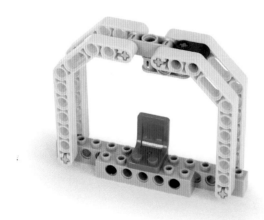

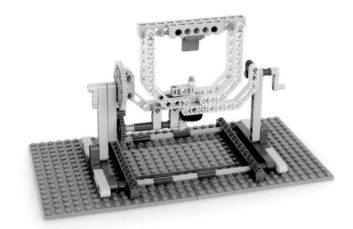

STEP 27: Attach a chair to the frame.

STEP 28: Attach the chair frame to the dark tan axle that is hanging down from the 20-tooth Technic bevel gear. Secure it with a yellow Technic bush (½ length).

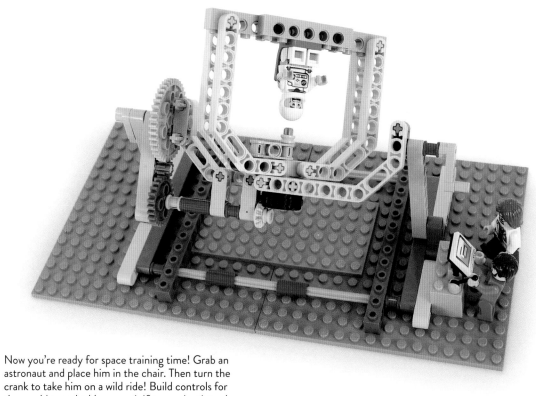

Now you're ready for space training time! Grab an astronaut and place him in the chair. Then turn the crank to take him on a wild ride! Build controls for the machine and add some minifigure scientists who are operating the controls.

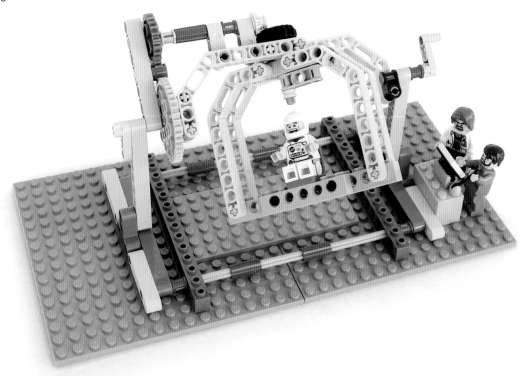

ROCKET LAUNCH PAD

Everyone's favorite station at Space Training Camp is definitely the Rocket Launch Pad! This station is equipped with a launch pad for the rockets and a control area for the scientists so that they can activate the rocket launch from behind a row of windows. It's definitely safer that way! The scientists can use the rockets to study flight and to gather information about outer space. (And apparently they can also get some practice with the fire extinguisher!)

PARTS LIST

DARK GRAY BRICKS
1—8 x 16 plate
1—4 x 12 plate
1—2 x 10 plate
1—1 x 8 plate
1—1 x 2 plate
1—1 x 2 brick
1—1 x 8 brick
2—4 x 4 round plates
1—2 x 2 round plate
2—4 x 4 round bricks
1—4 x 4 x 2 cone
4—arms, mechanical (LEGO ID 53989)

LIGHT GRAY BRICKS
1—2 x 10 brick
1—2 x 8 brick
5—2 x 4 bricks
4—2 x 2 bricks
1—6 x 6 plate
3—2 x 2 plates
4—2 x 4 tiles
1—2 x 2 tile
1—4 x 4 round plate

BLUE BRICKS
2—1 x 3 bricks
3—1 x 4 bricks
6—1 x 6 bricks
1—1 x 2 brick
4—2 x 2 round bricks

ASSORTED BRICKS
2—2 x 2 slopes with screens and controls
2—levers (antennas)
1—1 x 2 hinge brick with 2 x 2 hinge plate
2—1 x 2 tiles with a computer keyboard
1—1 x 2 tile with gauges
1—2 x 2 tile with computer screen
3—white chairs
3—3 x 4 x 4 translucent light blue windshields, inverted
1—2 x 2 black plate, modified with an octagonal bar frame
1—2 x 2 x 2 red cone

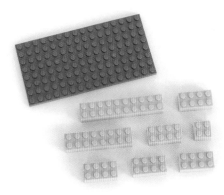

STEP 1: Build the base for the mission control area. Grab an 8 x 16 plate and the bricks shown. If you don't have a plate that large, connect some smaller ones.

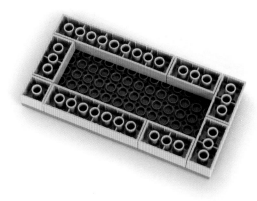

STEP 2: Build a layer of bricks around the perimeter of the underside of the 8 x 16 plate.

STEP 3: Flip the base over and add two rows of blue bricks on three sides of the building. It's easier to play with the mission control if you leave the back open.

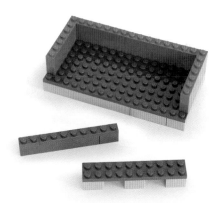

STEP 4: Build a desk area. Place a 1 x 8 plate and a 1 x 2 plate on top of a 1 x 8 brick and a 1 x 2 brick. Then grab a 2 x 10 plate. Support it with three 2 x 2 bricks underneath.

STEP 5: Attach the desk inside the building. Then grab some bricks for building computer screens, buttons and controls. If you don't have the exact bricks shown, get creative with what you have.

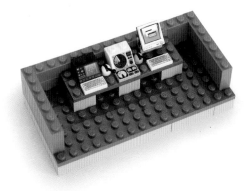

STEP 6: Place the computer screens and the controls on the desk to create three workstations.

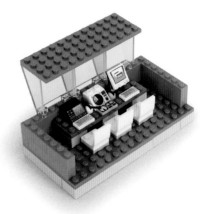

STEP 7: Three inverted windshields make a cool row of windows for the building! Add chairs with a 2 x 2 plate under each one.

STEP 8: Place a 4 x 12 plate over the windshields to create a partial roof.

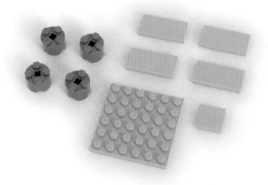

STEP 9: Gather the bricks shown for building the rocket launch pad. The launch pad does not have to have tiles on top of it if you don't have those. They do make the rocket sit more evenly on the launch pad, but you can make do without them.

STEP 10: Attach the tiles to the 6 x 6 plate, and then put a 2 x 2 round brick under each corner.

STEP 11: Build the rocket! Grab the bricks shown.

STEP 12: Attach each mechanical arm to the 2 x 2 plate with an octagonal bar. Then place a 2 x 2 round plate on top.

STEP 13: Place three 4 x 4 round plates on top of the base.

STEP 14: Complete the rocket with three 4 x 4 round bricks, a 4 x 4 cone and a 2 x 2 cone. Use whichever colors you like!

Now you're ready to launch your first rocket! Add some scientists working in the mission control center.

UM, GUYS! CAN I GET A LITTLE HELP OUT HERE?

Wow, that wasn't supposed to happen! Good thing the scientists were paying attention and had a fire extinguisher handy. Hopefully that little extinguisher will be enough to put out the fire!

ALIEN HEADQUARTERS

Jay Zebulon was flying his Z-3 Explorer toward home when something darted into his path. Crash! The collision was unavoidable. It was Krayzon, leader of the Bardenoids. Krayzon was zooming along in his flying saucer, not looking where he was going, as usual. Jay jumped out of his ship to assess the damage. He could tell in three seconds that he wasn't going anywhere anytime soon—at least not in THAT spaceship!

"You should look where you are going!" squeaked Krayzon.

"I should . . . ? Don't you mean YOU should look where you're going?" Jay exploded.

While he was formulating a plan for what to do next, Jay heard a rumbling sound. He looked up and saw a giant battle tank rolling toward him. Oh great! The Bardenoids had built a tank! He wasn't sure what that tank was for, but it couldn't be good. He was going to have to figure out a way to get off this planet . . . and fast!

Create epic scenes with astronauts and aliens! If you don't have any alien minifigures, that's no problem at all. Construct your own awesome alien creatures, and then create amazing space vehicles.

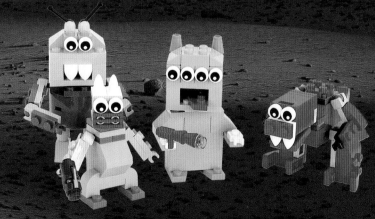

ALIEN SPEEDERS

Humans and aliens may disagree on a lot of things, but speeder races are one thing that everyone can enjoy. Tickets sell quickly to watch Gardon or Eskelon take on one of the human pilots. The winner gets bragging rights and a privileged position at the next race. You will love building these speeders! These one-person space vehicles are like motorized bicycles that can FLY. Once you've built a few different speeder designs, you'll want to set up a race course with a finish line and benches for the audience to sit on.

PARTS LIST

LIGHT GRAY BRICKS
1—2 x 6 brick
1—2 x 2 plate
1—1 x 2–1 x 2 bracket, inverted
1—2 x 2 plate with a pinhole
1—2 x 2 flag
2—1 x 2 plates with a socket on the end
2—1 x 2 grills
1—1 x 2 plate with one stud on top
1—2 x 2 truncated cone
1—handlebar
1—1 x 1 tile with a clip on top
1—wheel with a pinhole

DARK GRAY BRICKS
2—2 x 6 plates
1—1 x 4 plate
1—2 x 2 plate

ORANGE BRICKS
2—2 x 2 slopes
1—2 x 2 brick
1—2 x 3 wedge plate, right
1—2 x 3 wedge plate, left
1—2 x 2 inverted slope

WHITE BRICKS
1—1 x 2 plate
1—1 x 2–1 x 2 bracket

2—1 x 6 inverted curved slopes
1—1 x 2 grill
1—1 x 2 plate with two clips on the side
1—6 x 2 wedge, right
1—6 x 2 wedge, left

BLACK BRICKS
1—1 x 2 plate with a handle on the side
1—1 x 2 plate with a handle on the side, free ends
1—2 x 3 plate
1—Technic pin with friction ridges

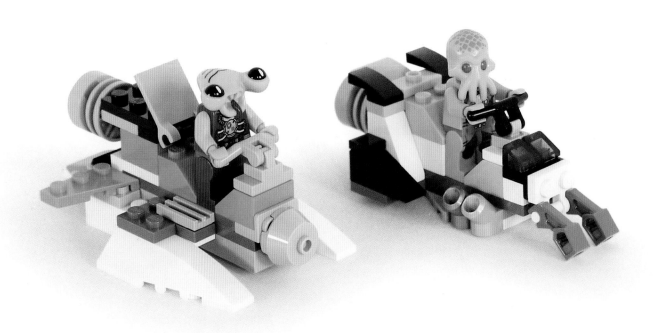

STEP 1: Start with a 2 x 6 light gray brick.

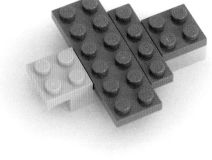

STEP 2: Add a 2 x 2 light gray plate, a 2 x 6 dark gray plate, a 1 x 4 dark gray plate and a 2 x 2 dark gray plate. The light gray plate will hang halfway off the 2 x 6 light gray brick.

STEP 3: Place a 2 x 6 dark gray plate and a 1 x 2—1 x 2 light gray bracket (inverted) in the center.

STEP 4: Place a 1 x 2—1 x 2 white bracket and a 1 x 2 white plate on the back of the speeder. Then add two 2 x 2 orange slopes as shown.

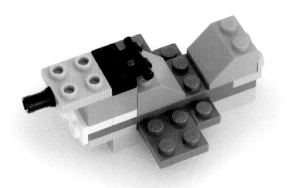

STEP 5: Attach a 2 x 2 orange brick. Then add a 1 x 2 black plate with a handle (free ends) and a 2 x 2 light gray plate with a pinhole. Insert a black pin into the pinhole.

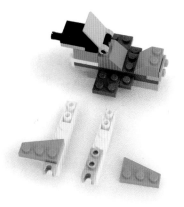

STEP 6: Place a 2 x 3 black plate on the back. Then attach a 2 x 2 light gray flag to the handle on the 1 x 2 black plate. Find two 1 x 6 white curved inverted slopes, and add a 1 x 2 light gray plate with a socket on the end and a 2 x 3 orange wedge plate to each one.

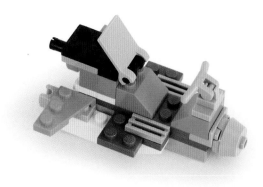

STEP 7: Attach the white inverted curved slopes to the underside of the dark gray plates on each side of the speeder. Then gather the bricks shown.

STEP 8: Use a 1 x 2 light gray plate with one stud on top and a 1 x 1 light gray tile with a clip to attach the handlebars to the speeder. Add a 1 x 2 light gray grill on each side, and place the 2 x 2 light gray cone on the front.

STEP 9: Turn the speeder around. Attach a 1 x 2 black plate with a handle to a 2 x 2 orange inverted slope. Then add a 1 x 2 white grill.

STEP 10: Use a 1 x 2 white plate with two clips on the side to attach this to the back end of the speeder. You can pivot the orange inverted slope to just the right angle.

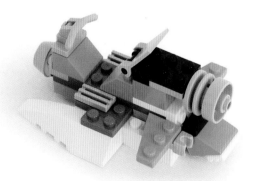

STEP 11: Finish up the speeder by adding a 6 x 2 wedge on each side and attaching a wheel to the black pin. Your speeder is complete!

Find an alien who's ready to go for a test drive!

Now that you've got the idea, try modifying the design to build more speeders. This speeder has two 1 x 4 plates with exhaust tubes under the main body. Mechanical arms give the front a fun look.

The base of this speeder is a 2 x 8 plate. Add a 2 x 6 plate perpendicular to the 2 x 8 plate, and you've got a great platform for adding bricks and slopes to make the speeder look really terrific!

See if you can use the photos to create this type of speeder as well. This one has the driver seated rather than standing. The seat is a 2 x 2 light gray plate modified with grills.

Bricks and plates with clips and handles are very useful for attaching things, such as the taillights. The lights on the front of the speeder are attached to a 1 x 2 light gray plate with handles.

Once your fleet of speeders is complete, try building a race track! Attach black and white 2 x 2 plates to a long, dark gray plate to create a finish line. Use bricks to build stands for the audience to sit on, and then set up a race-to-the-finish scene! Clear bricks work well when you are posing flying vehicles. Placing a couple under each speeder will make them look like they are hovering.

Try setting up a scene where aliens are zooming through the trees on their speeders! The space pilots found a good hiding place among the trees. They'd rather not be discovered by Gardon!

ASTRO-BOTS

Build some adorable one-eyed aliens! These curious little creatures hide in the crevices of space rocks and then sneak up on intruders, like astronauts, when they least expect it. Their tiny hands can hold a space blaster or any minifigure tool. Use bricks in your favorite colors for this project. You'll want to assemble several of these fun Astro-Bots for creating awesome space scenes!

PARTS LIST

1—1 x 2 black plate with a handle
1—2 x 2 black round plate modified with octagonal bars
1—2 x 2 turntable
4—1 x 1 brown slopes, 30 degree
2—1 x 1 lime green slopes, 30 degree

1— lever (antenna) in any color
1—1 x 1 dark gray brick with studs on 4 sides
1—1 x 1 translucent blue round tile (or use another color)
1—2 x 2 dark gray round plate
2—1 x 1 lime green round plates

2—1 x 1 white plates
2—1 x 1 light gray bricks with a clip on the side
2—1 x 1 dark gray tiles with a clip on top
2—1 x 1 light gray plates with a clip, horizontal or vertical

STEP 1: Gather the bricks shown for building the Astro-Bot's head.

STEP 2: Attach the open stud on the top of the 1 x 1 dark gray brick to the handle on the black plate.

STEP 3: Add a light gray lever (antenna).

STEP 4: Build the face by attaching a 1 x 1 translucent blue round tile and two 1 x 1 lime green slopes (30 degree). Substitute other colors if needed.

STEP 5: Attach the two 1 x 1 brown slopes to the black plate. Then attach the head to a 2 x 2 turntable.

STEP 6: Gather the bricks shown for building the Astro-Bot's body.

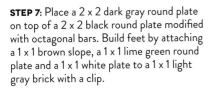

STEP 7: Place a 2 x 2 dark gray round plate on top of a 2 x 2 black round plate modified with octagonal bars. Build feet by attaching a 1 x 1 brown slope, a 1 x 1 lime green round plate and a 1 x 1 white plate to a 1 x 1 light gray brick with a clip.

STEP 8: Attach the head to the body. Then attach the feet to the black bars on the body. Find two 1 x 1 dark gray tiles with a clip on top and two 1 x 1 light gray plates with a clip for building hands.

STEP 9: Place one 1 x 1 dark gray tile with a clip on each light gray plate.

STEP 10: Attach the hands to the body. You can use clips with either a horizontal or vertical orientation when building the hands. If you want your Astro-Bot to hold a space blaster, he'll need at least one hand with a horizontal clip.

IT'S OKAY, I'M OUT OF HERE! NO REASON TO BE UPSET!

Now build more Astro-Bots in other colors! It's amazing how much personality you can achieve with just a few bricks.

Pretend that one of your astronauts is exploring a new planet and unexpectedly finds himself being attacked by some Astro-Bots! Yikes!

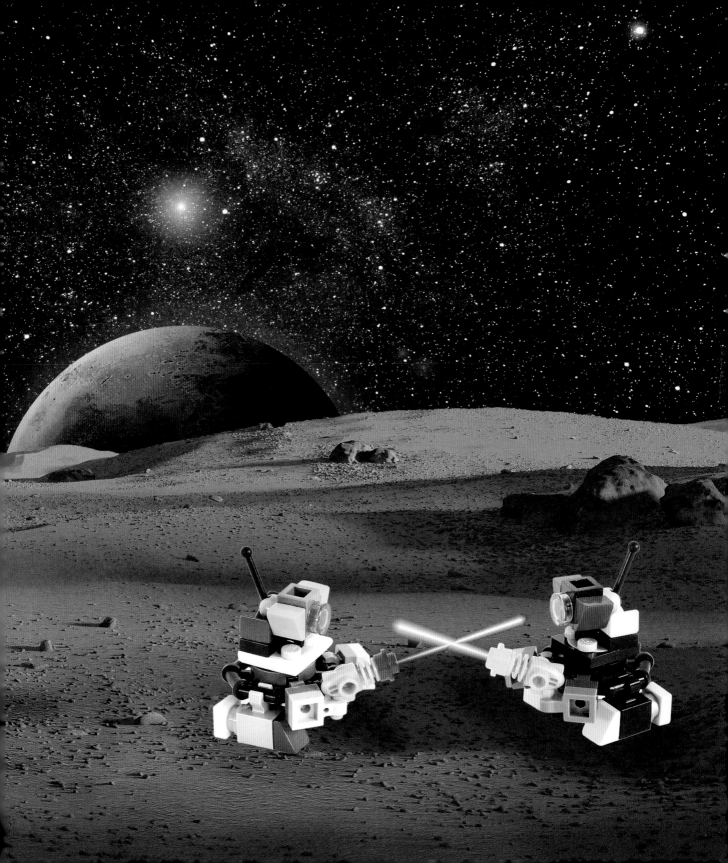

EPIC BATTLE TANK

The building of this battle tank was prompted by Captain Kramer's lockdown on all criminal alien activity. Not wanting to be told what to do, Krayzon, the Bardenoids' leader, commanded that new defense vehicles be constructed. Sturdy treads allow the tank to rumble across a rocky planet surface, and posable blasters make it a formidable threat to enemies. If you don't have the exact bricks shown, get creative with what you have. The windshield can be replaced with a different type, and you can use wheels instead of tracks, if needed.

PARTS LIST

LIGHT GRAY BRICKS
1—6 x 10 plate
1—2 x 4 wedge plate
2—1 x 2 bricks, two bricks high
2—1 x 2 slopes
4—1 x 1 bricks
2—1 x 3 plates
1—1 x 2 plate with a socket on the side
2—1 x 4 antennas
4—Technic bushes
1—wheel with a pinhole

DARK GRAY BRICKS
1—1 x 8 plate
3—2 x 2 plates
1—1 x 4 plate
1—1 x 4 Technic brick
1—1 x 4 tile
1—1 x 2—2 x 2 bracket
1—1 x 2 plate with one stud on top
1—1 x 2 plate with a ball on the side
2—1 x 2 slopes, 30 degree
2—1 x 1 slopes, 30 degree
1—1 x 1 tile with a clip on top
1—1 x 1 round brick with fins
1—1 x 1 cone
2—1 x 1 round plates

2—1 x 2 grills
1—pneumatic hose connector with axle connector
4—Technic gears, 24 tooth
1—handlebar

BLACK BRICKS
2—1 x 10 Technic bricks
2—Technic axles, 10 studs long
1—1 x 6 brick
4—1 x 4 bricks
2—2 x 6 plates
1—1 x 6 plate
2—1 x 1 bricks
1—1 x 2 brick
2—1 x 3 curved slopes
2—1 x 2 plates with a handle on the side, free ends
2—1 x 2 plates with a clip on the end
1—1 x 2 tile
1—1 x 2 plate with one stud on top
1—1 x 2 grill
2—1 x 1 slopes, 30 degree
1—1 x 1 tile with a clip on top
64—Technic track links

WHITE BRICKS
1—6 x 6 plate
3—1 x 6 plates
1—1 x 4 plate

2—1 x 3 plates
4—1 x 2 plates
1—1 x 2 plate with two clips on the side
1—6 x 8 Technic brick with an open center
1—2 x 8 x 2 boat window

LIME GREEN BRICKS
1—2 x 6 plate
1—2 x 3 plate
1—2 x 2 plate
1—1 x 6 brick
2—2 x 3 wedge plates, right
2—2 x 3 wedge plates, left
2—1 x 2 slopes
3—2 x 2 curved slopes
1—2 x 2 tile
1—1 x 2 tile
2—1 x 2 plates with one stud on top

ASSORTED BRICKS
4—1 x 2 x 2 clear panels
1—1 x 1 translucent red round plate
2—1 x 1 translucent blue round plates
1—1 x 1 translucent yellow round plate
2—1 x 1 translucent yellow plates
1—1 x 1 translucent green round plate
1—2 x 2 neon yellow dish
1—blue Technic pin, 3 studs long

STEP 1: Gather the bricks shown for building the base of the tank.

STEP 2: Attach the 2 x 6 lime green plate to the center of the underside of the 6 x 6 white plate.

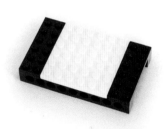

STEP 3: Attach the 6 x 6 white plate and two 2 x 6 black plates to two 1 x 10 black Technic bricks.

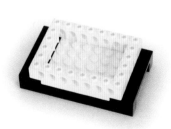

STEP 4: Add a 6 x 8 white Technic brick with an open center.

STEP 5: Place a 1 x 6 black plate on one end and a 1 x 6 white plate on the other end. Then gather the bricks shown.

STEP 6: Attach a 1 x 1 black brick, a 1 x 4 black brick and a 1 x 2 light gray brick (two bricks high) on each side.

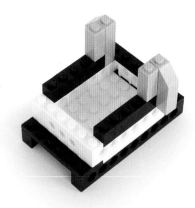

STEP 7: Place a 1 x 2 light gray slope on top of each 1 x 2 light gray brick. Then add two 1 x 1 light gray bricks just behind that on each side of the tank.

STEP 8: Gather the bricks shown.

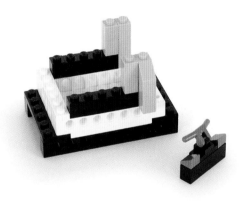

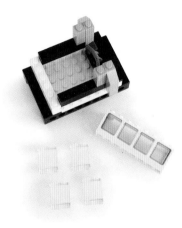

STEP 9: Attach a 1 x 2 black plate with one stud on top and a 1 x 1 black tile with a clip on top to a 1 x 4 black brick. Use these to hold the handlebars. Then add two 1 x 1 dark gray slopes (30 degree).

STEP 10: Place the handlebars inside the tank. Then find a 2 x 8 x 2 boat window and four 1 x 2 x 2 clear panels. If you don't have these, substitute other windows.

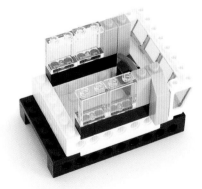

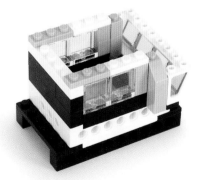

STEP 11: Attach the windows as shown.

STEP 12: Add a 1 x 6 black brick, a 1 x 4 black brick and a 1 x 2 black brick on the back of the tank. Then add two 1 x 6 white plates on top. Place a 1 x 3 light gray plate and a 1 x 3 white plate on each side above the clear panels.

STEP 13: Place a 1 x 8 dark gray plate on the front of the tank, and add a 1 x 2 black plate with a clip behind it on each side. Then find the bricks shown.

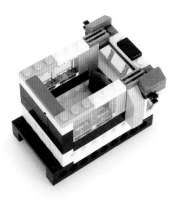

STEP 14: Place a 2 x 2 dark gray plate in each front corner. Then add the 1 x 2 slopes (30 degree) and the 1 x 2 grills. Place a 1 x 4 white plate in the front and center of the tank. Then add a 1 x 2 black tile on top of that. Place the 1 x 4 dark gray tile on the back.

STEP 15: Find two 1 x 2 lime green slopes and four 1 x 2 white plates.

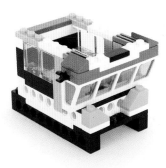

STEP 16: Attach each 1 x 2 lime green slope to a 1 x 2 white plate, and place these on the front of the tank. Then place the other two 1 x 2 white plates on the top of the tank on either side of the black tile.

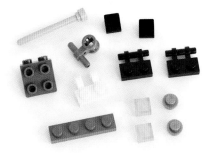

STEP 17: Gather the bricks shown.

STEP 18: Place a 1 x 1 translucent yellow plate and a 1 x 1 dark gray round plate on top of each 1 x 2 black plate with a handle on the side (free ends).

STEP 19: Attach both black plates to the 1 x 4 dark gray plate. Then attach two 1 x 1 black slopes (30 degree) to a 1 x 2 white plate with two clips on the side.

STEP 20: Place the 1 x 2 white plate with clips on top of the dark gray 1 x 2—2 x 2 bracket. Then insert a Technic pneumatic hose connector with axle connector into the clips.

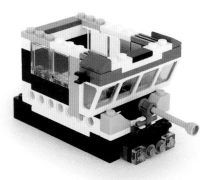

STEP 21: Attach the 1 x 4 plate with the headlights to the bracket. Insert the 1 x 4 antenna into the axle connector to create the tank's blaster.

STEP 22: Place the blaster and headlight assembly on the front of the tank in between the two 1 x 2 lime green bricks.

STEP 23: Turn the tank around to the back, and find the bricks shown.

STEP 24: Place a 1 x 4 dark gray Technic brick on the back of the tank. Insert a blue pin (3 studs long) into the center hole of the Technic brick. It will go through the white Technic brick that's behind it as well.

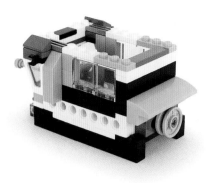

STEP 25: Slide a wheel with a pinhole onto the blue pin. Then attach the 1 x 6 lime green brick and three 2 x 2 curved slopes above the wheel.

STEP 26: Grab a 6 x 10 plate. Decorate it with the plates and tiles shown, or create your own design.

STEP 27: Place a red and green 1 x 1 translucent round plate under each of the 2 x 3 lime green plates that stick out from the sides of the ship. Then add the 2 x 2 lime green tile and the 1 x 2 black grill.

STEP 28: Attach the bricks shown to the end of a 1 x 4 light gray antenna. Attach a 1 x 2 light gray plate with a socket on the side to a 2 x 2 dark gray plate.

STEP 29: Place the two 1 x 3 black curved slopes on top of the plate with a socket. Then attach the 1 x 2 plate with one stud on top and the 1 x 1 tile with a clip to the 1 x 2 plate with a ball on the side.

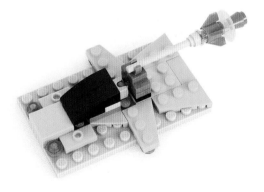

STEP 30: Attach the ball to the socket, and then attach the 2 x 2 dark gray plate to the roof of the ship. Attach the laser blaster to the clip.

STEP 31: Place the roof on top of the tank. The laser blaster should be able to move up and down and side to side.

STEP 32: Find four 24-tooth Technic gears, four light gray Technic bushes and two black axles (10 studs long).

STEP 33: Slide the axles through the black Technic bricks at the base of the tank. Place a light gray Technic bush on each end. Then slide a 24-tooth gear on each end.

STEP 34: Build two chains with 32 Technic track links in each. Wrap the tracks around the 24-tooth gears and then connect them. Your tank is complete! If you don't have tracks, try building your tank with rows of 3 or 4 wheels on each side.

Now it's time to create a battle scene between the aliens and humans! Grab one of your spaceships and pilots, such as Jay Zebulon and his Z-3 Explorer (page 48). Build some space rock formations for the minifigures to hide behind as they take aim with their space blasters.

FLYING SAUCERS

Captain Kramer was loading up his Sky Hawk for a flight back to Dexel. Just as he was closing the hatch, he could sense a round shadow overhead. Ugh, that had to be Blurgo, Krayzon's right-hand man in his flying saucer. "I wonder what he wants?" thought Kramer.

"Hello," barked Blurgo. "You not make Krayzon happy. . . ."

Build some classic disc-shaped UFOs for wacky space creatures to fly. Achieving the round shape can be a little challenging with LEGO bricks, but this unique design works well and looks fantastic. Build flying saucers with round corner bricks, or use round plates to create them.

MASTER KRAYZON, INTRUDERS HAVE BEEN SIGHTED IN SECTOR 12.

LAUNCHING MISSION TO ELIMINATE INTRUDERS IMMEDIATELY!

PARTS LIST

DARK GRAY BRICKS
2—6 x 6 plates
2—2 x 10 plates
1—2 x 4 plate
1—2 x 3 plate
3—1 x 4 plates
1—2 x 4 brick
1—1 x 4 brick
1—6 x 2 wedge, right
1—6 x 2 wedge, left
1—2 x 3 wedge plate, right
1—2 x 3 wedge plate, left
2—2 x 3 slopes
3—3 x 3 dishes
2—1 x 2 slopes with four slots

LIGHT GRAY BRICKS
1—2 x 14 plate
1—1 x 6 plate

1—2 x 4 plate
1—3 x 6 wedge plate, right
1—3 x 6 wedge plate, left
1—1 x 4 Technic brick
1—2 x 4 brick
1—2 x 2 truncated cone
1—2 x 2 curved slope with lip, no studs
2—wheels with pinholes
1—lever (antenna)

WHITE BRICKS
1—2 x 6 plate
1—2 x 2 plate
1—2 x 3 wedge plate, right
1—2 x 3 wedge plate, left
1—1 x 2 plate with two clips on the side
2—6 x 1 curved slopes
2—6 x 1 curved slopes, inverted

MEDIUM AZURE BRICKS
2—6 x 6 round corner bricks
2—2 x 4 bricks
1—1 x 4 brick
1—1 x 6 plate
2—2 x 4 plates
1—1 x 4 curved slope

YELLOW BRICKS
2—1 x 6 plates
2—1 x 4 plates
1—1 x 4 tile
2—1 x 1 slopes, 30 degree
1—1 x 2 tile

ASSORTED BRICKS
1—black Technic pin, 3 studs long
1—1 x 2 slope with gauges
1—1 x 2 hinge brick and 2 x 2 hinge plate
1—1 x 1 translucent pink cone
1—6 x 4 windshield bubble canopy

STEP 1: Find two 6 x 6 dark gray plates and a 2 x 14 light gray plate.

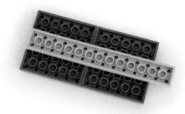

STEP 2: Use the 2 x 14 plate to connect the two 6 x 6 plates as shown.

STEP 3: Add two 2 x 4 medium azure plates so that they attach a 2 x 10 dark gray plate on each side. Then find the bricks shown.

STEP 4: Add a 2 x 3 dark gray wedge plate on each side. Then attach a 2 x 3 white wedge plate to each of these.

STEP 5: Turn the flying saucer over. Then find the bricks shown.

STEP 6: Add the 2 x 2 white plate to the front of the flying saucer. Then place two 3 x 6 light gray wedge plates and a 2 x 4 dark gray plate on the back.

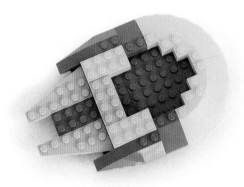

STEP 7: Place two 6 x 6 round corner bricks on the front of the ship. Then add a 2 x 3 dark gray slope on each side.

STEP 8: Add a 6 x 2 dark gray wedge on each side. Then add a 2 x 4 light gray brick and two 2 x 4 medium azure bricks in the middle as shown.

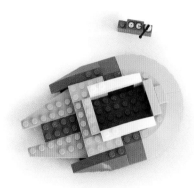

STEP 9: Place a 1 x 4 yellow plate, two 6 x 1 white curved slopes, a 1 x 4 yellow tile and a 1 x 2 yellow tile around the cockpit area. Then find a 1 x 4 dark gray brick and attach a 1 x 2 slope with gauges and a lever (antenna).

STEP 10: Place the controls inside the cockpit. Attach a 1 x 6 yellow plate and a 1 x 1 yellow slope (30 degree) on each side. On the back, add a 2 x 6 white plate. Place a 1 x 6 medium azure plate and a 1 x 4 dark gray plate on top of the white plate.

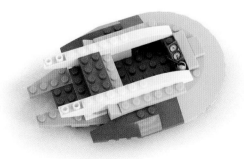

STEP 11: Add a 2 x 4 dark gray brick behind the cockpit area. Then add a 6 x 1 white inverted curved slope on each side.

STEP 12: Place a 1 x 4 light gray Technic brick on the back of the ship. Then find the bricks shown.

STEP 13: Attach the two 1 x 4 dark gray plates, 2 x 4 light gray plate and 1 x 6 light gray plate on the back of the flying saucer as shown. Then gather the bricks pictured.

STEP 14: Slide both wheels onto the black pin. Then place the 1 x 2 dark gray slopes with four slots on each of the white curved slopes. Add the 2 x 3 dark gray plate in the center of the back of the flying saucer.

STEP 15: Insert the black pin into the center of the Technic brick on the back of the ship, and then attach the 2 x 2 light gray curved slope (with a lip). Then find the bricks shown for building the windshield and blaster. The windshield is a 6 x 4 bubble canopy.

STEP 16: Attach a 2 x 2 light gray truncated cone to a hinge brick. Then add a translucent pink cone. Place a 1 x 4 medium azure brick on top of a 1 x 4 yellow plate. Add a 1 x 2 white plate with two clips on the side and a 1 x 4 medium azure curved slope on top of that.

STEP 17: Place the laser blaster and hinge brick on the ship. Then attach the windshield.

STEP 18: Place three 3 x 3 dark gray dishes on the underside of the ship. Your flying saucer is complete!

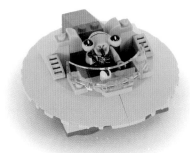

If you don't have the 6 x 6 round corner bricks used for building the front of the flying saucer, you can build this type of flying saucer with 4 x 4 round corner plates.

The base of the flying saucer is built from four 4 x 4 round corner plates. There are four 4 x 4 round corner bricks on top of that, which leaves an opening in the center for the alien driver to sit.

Another option is to build a flying saucer with an open top. This design uses four 6 x 6 round corner bricks to create a classic flying saucer shape.

Use a 4 x 4 wedge to create a cool looking tail on the back of the flying saucer. The great thing about alien vehicles is that you can dream up any design you like! Modify any of these flying saucer designs with the bricks you have to make something really great.

Then create a scene! Pretend that two of your pilots are being chased because the Bardenoids think they have stolen some important battle plans. But they haven't. . . . Now they have to plot their escape!

CRAGULONS

Cragulons are pesky (and slightly crazy) space aliens who live on the planet Craggle. Thankfully, most of their troublesome plots don't work out (they're not the smartest creatures), but they sure can be a pain! Give your Cragulons two eyes or a whole bunch. Build a silly mouth with a tongue hanging out, or give your Cragulon crazy big teeth. Plates with balls and sockets make great posable arm joints, and plates with clips make the perfect hands for holding space blasters.

PARTS LIST FOR BUILDING THE LIME GREEN CRAGULON

LIME GREEN BRICKS
4—2 x 4 plates
4—1 x 4 plates
1—1 x 4 brick
2—1 x 2 bricks
4—1 x 1 bricks with a stud on the side
3—2 x 4 bricks

3—1 x 2 slopes, 30 degree
2—2 x 2 plates
1—2 x 2 brick
2—2 x 2 slopes

ASSORTED BRICKS
1—2 x 3 red wedge plate, right
2—1 x 1 orange cones
4—eyes

1—2 x 2 turntable
1—2 x 3 orange wedge plate, right
1—2 x 3 orange wedge plate, left
2—1 x 1 white plates with a clip, vertical
1—red minifigure megaphone
1—1 x 1 red cone
1—1 x 1 translucent light blue round plate

STEP 1: Build the lime green Cragulon! Grab the bricks shown.

STEP 2: Place two 1 x 2 bricks on the edges of a 2 x 4 plate. Then attach a 2 x 3 red wedge plate to be a tongue.

STEP 3: Attach a 1 x 4 brick to a 1 x 4 plate, and line them up next to the tongue. They are not attached to the head yet.

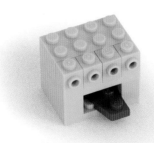

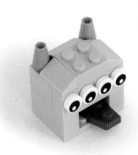

STEP 4: Connect the two parts of the head with a 2 x 4 plate and a 1 x 4 plate.

STEP 5: Add four 1 x 1 bricks with a stud on the side. Then add a 2 x 4 brick behind them.

STEP 6: Attach eyes to the bricks with a stud on the side. Then place two 2 x 2 plates on top of the head. Add three 1 x 2 slopes (30 degree) and two 1 x 1 orange cones.

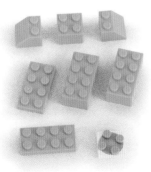

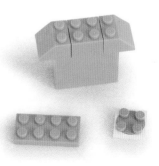

STEP 7: Gather the bricks shown for building the body.

STEP 8: Build a tower with a 2 x 4 plate and two 2 x 4 bricks. Then add two 2 x 2 slopes and a 2 x 2 brick.

STEP 9: Place a 2 x 4 plate and a 2 x 2 turntable on top of the body. Find the bricks shown.

STEP 10: Add a 1 x 4 plate under each 2 x 2 slope to create arms. Then attach 1 x 1 white plates with a clip to be hands. Build the feet by putting two 2 x 3 orange wedge plates under the body.

STEP 11: Attach the head to the turntable on the body, and your Cragulon is complete!

STEP 12: Build a quick space blaster with a red megaphone brick, a 1 x 1 red cone and a 1 x 1 translucent blue round plate.

Your Cragulon can easily hold the space blaster with his clip hands! His many eyes and silly tongue make him look so funny!

Now experiment with more Cragulon designs. This one has two 1 x 1 white plates with a vertical tooth attached to the top of his mouth. Use 1 x 2 plates with balls and sockets to create posable arm joints.

Build a tiny Cragulon with a spiky head made out of plates with teeth.

He can easily turn his head because it's mounted on a turntable.

This funny Cragulon has a container for a head! Open the container door, and his mouth is open.

Give this Cragulon dinosaur-style legs and arms, and build a tail with spikes. There are joints at the hips, shoulders, tail and neck, so he is easy to pose.

HELLO. I AM A FRIENDLY VISITOR! WHAT IS YOUR NAME?

GLUMP WUGGA BIM. MUGGA BOO!

Pretend that one of your space pilots has landed on Craggle and is discovering the Cragulons for the first time. And . . . they're having a little bit of trouble understanding each other!

TURBO BOOSTER ALIEN SHIP

Once you've created some Cragulons (page 108), build them a zippy spaceship! The Cragulons can fit inside this ship to drive it, thanks to the open roof. You may want to build more than one so that your aliens can travel together and battle with the humans! They are always devising plots, such as blocking human space travel and intercepting important shipments.

PARTS LIST

DARK GRAY BRICKS
1—8 x 8 plate
1—4 x 10 plate
1—2 x 10 plate
3—2 x 8 plates
1—4 x 6 plate
1—2 x 4 plate
2—1 x 4 plates
2—1 x 2 plates
1—1 x 6 brick
1—1 x 4 brick with 4 studs on the side
2—1 x 2 Technic bricks with axle holes
1—1 x 2—1 x 2 hinge plate
1—1 x 2 grill

BLUE BRICKS
2—1 x 8 bricks
1—1 x 6 brick
2—1 x 4 bricks
2—3 x 6 wedge plates, right
2—3 x 6 wedge plates, left
2—1 x 8 plates

1—1 x 6 plate
2—2 x 3 inverted slopes
1—2 x 2 inverted slope
1—6 x 2 wedge, right
1—6 x 2 wedge, left

WHITE BRICKS
2—8 x 8 wedge plates, cut corners
2—2 x 6 plates
3—1 x 6 plates
4—1 x 4 plates
2—1 x 2 plates
1—2 x 6 brick
3—2 x 2 slopes
1—4 x 4 x ⅔ wedge, triple curved
1—1 x 1 tile with a clip on top

LIGHT GRAY BRICKS
3—1 x 4 bricks with 4 studs on the side
1—2 x 4 brick
3—2 x 2 bricks
2—2 x 2 round bricks with ridges
2—6 x 1 inverted wedges, right
2—6 x 1 inverted wedges, left

1—handlebars
1—lever (antenna)
1—1 x 2 grill

MEDIUM AZURE BRICKS
4—1 x 4 bricks
2—1 x 2 bricks
6—1 x 2 slopes
2—1 x 1 bricks
1—1 x 6 plate

ASSORTED BRICKS
1—5 x 8 x 2 translucent light blue windshield
1—1 x 6 black plate
2—1 x 1 translucent red round tiles
1—1 x 1 translucent red round plate
1—1 x 1 translucent red round brick
2—1 x 1 translucent orange round tiles
1—1 x 1 translucent orange plate
1—1 x 1 translucent neon green round plate
2—red Technic axles, 2 studs long with notches

STEP 1: Grab the dark gray plates shown for building the base of the ship.

STEP 2: Use the 4 x 6 plate and the 2 x 4 plate to join the other three plates.

STEP 3: Turn the ship over and gather the plates shown.

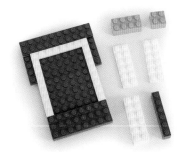

STEP 4: Place a 2 x 10 dark gray plate on the front of the ship. Then add a 2 x 8 dark gray plate and two 1 x 4 dark gray plates on the back. Attach a 1 x 6 white plate on each side.

STEP 5: Place two 1 x 4 white plates and two 1 x 2 white plates on the ship. Then gather the bricks shown.

STEP 6: Fill in the front of the ship with a 1 x 6 dark gray brick, a 2 x 4 light gray brick, a 2 x 2 light gray brick and a 2 x 6 white brick.

STEP 7: Place two 2 x 6 white plates on top of the 2 x 6 white brick.

STEP 8: Gather the bricks shown for building the cockpit controls.

STEP 9: Stack two 1 x 4 white plates and then add a 1 x 4 dark gray brick with 4 studs on the side. Place a 1 x 2 dark gray grill on top of that.

STEP 10: Attach translucent plates, a lever (antenna) and a 1 x 1 white tile with a clip on top to the dark gray brick with 4 studs on the side. Add the handlebars to the white tile with a clip.

STEP 11: Add the cockpit controls to the ship. Then add a 1 x 2 light gray grill, a 1 x 1 translucent neon green round plate and a 1 x 1 translucent red round brick.

STEP 12: Turn the ship around and add two 1 x 4 light gray bricks with 4 studs on the side to the front of the ship. Then place a 1 x 8 blue brick and a 1 x 4 blue brick on each side of the ship. Gather the bricks shown.

STEP 13: Attach the 1 x 6 black plate and the 1 x 6 blue plate as shown. Then add a 1 x 1 translucent red round tile on each side of the blue plate.

STEP 14: Place three 2 x 2 white slopes across the front of the ship. Then add a 1 x 2 medium azure slope, two 1 x 4 medium azure bricks and a 1 x 2 medium azure brick on each side. Find the bricks shown.

STEP 15: Attach the 1 x 6 blue brick and 1 x 6 medium azure plate to the back of the spaceship.

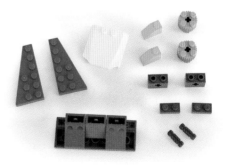

STEP 16: Gather the bricks shown for building the fins and engines on the back of the ship.

STEP 17: Attach two 2 x 3 blue inverted slopes and one 2 x 2 blue inverted slope to the underside of a 2 x 8 dark gray plate and a 1 x 8 blue plate.

STEP 18: Turn the plates over and add a 3 x 6 wedge plate on each side. Then place a 4 x 4 x ⅔ white wedge (triple curved) in the middle.

STEP 19: Attach a 1 x 2 dark gray Technic brick with an axle hole to each 1 x 2 dark gray plate. Insert a red axle (2 studs long) into each Technic brick. Then attach a 1 x 2 medium azure slope to each side of the fins.

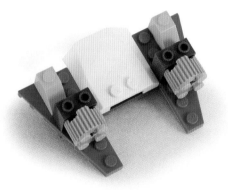

STEP 20: Slide a 2 x 2 light gray round brick with ridges onto each red axle. Then attach the 1 x 2 dark gray bricks to the fins.

STEP 21: Connect the fins to the back of the ship. Then gather the bricks shown.

STEP 22: Attach the 1 x 4 light gray brick with 4 studs on the side to the blue plate on the front of the ship. Then attach a 1 x 8 blue plate to the studs that are on the side of the light gray brick.

STEP 23: Place a 1 x 6 white plate on the front of the ship. Use 1 x 1 translucent orange tiles for headlights, and place a 1 x 2—1 x 2 dark gray hinge plate in between them. Or substitute the hinge plate with two 1 x 2 grills.

STEP 24: Build the wings. Each wing has an 8 x 8 white wedge plate with cut corners, a 6 x 2 blue wedge, a 3 x 6 blue wedge plate, a 1 x 2 medium azure slope and a 1 x 1 medium azure brick. If you don't have the exact bricks shown, modify the wing to create your own design.

STEP 25: Attach the wings to the dark gray plates that stick out on each side of the ship.

STEP 26: Place the windshield on the ship. The one pictured is a 5 x 8 x 2 windshield. Substitute a different windshield shape if needed.

STEP 27: Turn the ship upside down and grab four 6 x 2 light gray inverted wedges and two 2 x 2 bricks.

STEP 28: Use these bricks to give the bottom of the ship more depth. Your Turbo Booster Alien Ship is complete!

Time for a test drive! Most of the Cragulons, with the exception of the red dinosaur-like design, will fit inside the cockpit of the ship. They look kind of hilarious with their heads sticking up out of the top!

SPACE LIFE

Marshall Grady wiped the sweat and dust from his face as he stood back to admire his progress. He had been drilling through solid rock for hours, and the work was only half done. Taming a new planet was challenging, but it would be worth it once the new space community was constructed. Just then, he saw a flash of green dart past him. It was Slimy Joe Zorgo—a known alien criminal! Slimy Joe had been stealing parts out of spaceships, rendering them useless until Jett could fix them up again at his repair dock. Such a pain!

Marshall turned to see what was going on. Officer Astrid Kenner was running after Joe—and she was gaining on him! In minutes, she had him in handcuffs. "That's the last time you'll be giving us any trouble!" Astrid yelled.

"Great job, Astrid!" called Marshall.

"Thanks!" she replied. "See you later out at the research station!"

Life in space sure was crazy! But Marshall loved the adventure.

Go beyond spaceships to create an entire space community. Learn how to build an incredible police spaceship and jail. Then construct a research center and some rugged all-terrain vehicles. Transport minifigures from one place to another in a hovering shuttle service. Then use these ideas as a springboard to create more space town creations!

POLICE CRUISER AND SPACE JAIL

Officers Carlos Gray and Astrid Kenner have one main goal: keeping the galaxy safe from criminals and nefarious creatures! The police cruiser is equipped with sirens and flashing lights, and no bad guy will be able to outrun (or outfly!) its powerful rocket engines. If there's trouble in space, the police are prepared to handle it!

BRING HIM ON IN, CARLOS. WE'VE BEEN TRYING TO TRACK DOWN SLIMY JOE ZORGO FOR A LONG TIME!

PARTS LIST
POLICE CRUISER SPACESHIP

WHITE BRICKS
1—2 x 6 plate
2—1 x 6 plates
1—2 x 4 plate
1—2 x 3 plate
1—2 x 2 plate
1—1 x 4 plate
1—3 x 6 wedge plate, right
1—3 x 6 wedge plate, left
1—2 x 3 wedge plate, right
1—2 x 3 wedge plate, left
1—6 x 2 wedge, right
1—6 x 2 wedge, left
1—8 x 3 wedge, right
1—8 x 3 wedge, left
2—1 x 3 curved slopes
1—2 x 2 curved slope
1—2 x 2 slope with controls
2—1 x 2 slopes, 30 degree
2—4 x 1 x 3 tails
2—chairs

DARK GRAY BRICKS
1—4 x 12 x ¾ vehicle base with a 4 x 2 recessed center
2—2 x 10 plates
1—2 x 8 plate
1—2 x 6 plate
2—1 x 6 plates
3—2 x 4 plates
2—1 x 4 plates
2—1 x 6 inverted curved slopes

1—1 x 2 brick
1—2 x 4 brick
4—1 x 2—1 x 2 brackets, inverted
2—1 x 2 plates with a clip on the end

LIGHT GRAY BRICKS
1—2 x 4 plate
2—1 x 4 plates
4—1 x 2—1 x 2 brackets, inverted
1—1 x 4 plate modified with angled tubes
1—2 x 2 curved slope
2—1 x 1 plates with a clip light
2—engines with a 2 x 2 top plate

BLACK BRICKS
1—2 x 4 wedge plate, right
1—2 x 4 wedge plate, left
1—2 x 2 curved slope
1—2 x 3 plate
2—2 x 4 plates
1—1 x 2 plate
1—1 x 4 curved slope
1—2 x 6 plate, round corner double

BLUE BRICKS
2—2 x 6 bricks
3—1 x 6 bricks
1—4 x 4 plate

ASSORTED BRICKS
1—1 x 2 translucent red brick
1—1 x 2 translucent blue brick
2—1 x 1 translucent red round plates
1—8 x 4 x 2 translucent light blue windshield with 4 studs and a handle

POLICE STATION BUILDING
1—32 x 32 light gray baseplate
Various dark gray bricks for building the walls
4—1 x 4 x 3 translucent light blue panels
2—3 x 4 x 4 translucent light blue windshields, inverted
Various light gray tiles (optional, for the top of the walls)
4—yellow chairs
1—1 x 4 x 6 door with police bars
1—1 x 4 x 6 door with translucent light blue window
1—1 x 4 x 3 window frame with bar window

BEDS
2—4 x 6 brown plates
8—1 x 1 brown round plates
4—2 x 4 light gray tiles
4—2 x 4 white plates

DESK
1—2 x 6 dark gray plate
1—2 x 4 dark gray plate
1—1 x 6 dark gray plate
1—1 x 4 dark gray plate
1—1 x 2 dark gray plate
1—1 x 6 dark gray brick
1—1 x 4 dark gray brick
2—2 x 4 light gray tiles
1—2 x 2 light gray tile
1—1 x 2 tile with a computer keyboard
1—2 x 2 black tile
1—1 x 2 hinge brick with 2 x 2 hinge plate

STEP 1: Grab a 4 x 12 x ¾ vehicle base with a 4 x 2 recessed center.

STEP 2: Attach a 2 x 6 white plate to the front of the vehicle base. Then add a 2 x 10 dark gray plate on each side and a 2 x 8 dark gray plate on the back. Then find two 2 x 4 black wedge plates.

STEP 3: Place the black wedge plates on the front of the spaceship as shown.

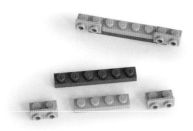

STEP 4: Attach two 1 x 2—1 x 2 light gray brackets (inverted) and a 1 x 4 light gray plate to a 1 x 6 dark gray plate. Make two of these.

STEP 5: Attach one of the plate-and-bracket assemblies to the underside of the ship on each side.

STEP 6: Gather the bricks shown for completing the bottom of the ship.

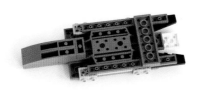

STEP 7: Place two 1 x 4 plates on the front of the ship with a 2 x 4 plate between them. Then add a 2 x 4 plate on the back.

STEP 8: Add the 2 x 6 plate across the front as shown. Place the two 1 x 6 inverted slope bricks and the 1 x 2 brick on the back end of the ship.

STEP 9: Turn the ship over. Add two 2 x 6 blue bricks and a 1 x 6 blue brick.

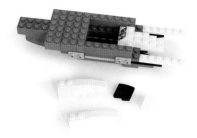

STEP 10: Place a 2 x 4 dark gray brick on the back of the ship. Then add a 1 x 6 blue brick and a 1 x 6 white plate on each side.

STEP 11: Gather the bricks shown.

STEP 12: Place a 2 x 4 white plate at the front of the cockpit and put a 2 x 2 slope with cockpit controls on top of it. Then add a 2 x 3 white plate and a 2 x 2 white plate in front of that.

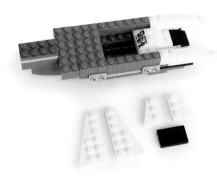

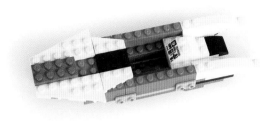

STEP 13: Stack a 2 x 4 light gray plate and a 2 x 4 dark gray plate and attach them to the back of the ship. Attach the 1 x 2 white slope right in front of the cockpit controls. Then add the 2 x 2 black curved slope and the 6 x 2 wedges to the front of the ship. Find the bricks shown.

STEP 14: Use the 3 x 6 white wedge plates to add shape to the back of the ship as shown. Then place a 2 x 3 black plate in between the 2 x 3 white wedge plates.

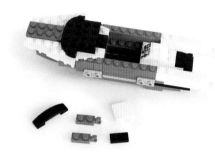

STEP 15: Gather the bricks shown.

STEP 16: Stack the 2 x 4 black plates and add them to the ship as shown. Place the 2 x 6 plate (round corner double) right behind them.

STEP 17: Attach the two 1 x 2 dark gray plates with a clip on the end to the top of the 2 x 4 black plates. Place a 1 x 2 black plate just behind them.

STEP 18: Add the 2 x 2 white curved slope and the 1 x 4 black curved slope so that they cover the dark gray plates with clips.

STEP 19: Place a 1 x 3 white curved slope on each side of the 2 x 2 white curved slope. Next, add a 1 x 4 light gray plate modified with angled tubes. Then find the bricks shown.

STEP 20: Attach the four 1 x 2—1 x 2 dark gray brackets to the back of the ship. Place the 1 x 4 white plate under the brackets where they hang off the edge of the ship.

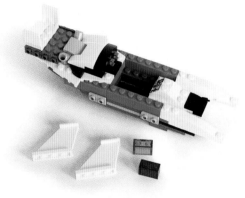

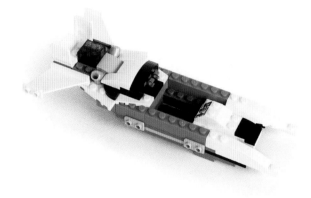

STEP 21: Place the 4 x 4 blue plate on top of the brackets. Then attach two white chairs and a 1 x 2 white slope (30 degree) on top of that. Add the 2 x 2 light gray curved slope on top of the exhaust tubes.

STEP 22: Use the brackets to attach a 4 x 1 x 3 tail on each side of the spaceship. Add a 1 x 2 translucent red brick and a 1 x 2 translucent blue brick to create police lights.

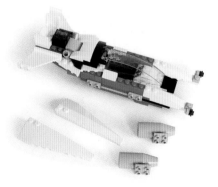

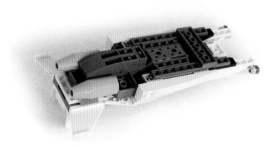

STEP 23: Attach an 8 x 4 x 2 windshield to the clips on the back of the cockpit area. Then find two 8 x 3 white wedges and two light gray engines with a 2 x 2 top plate.

STEP 24: Place the engines on the underside of the ship as shown.

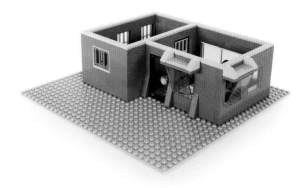

STEP 25: Attach the 8 x 3 white wedges to the brackets on the side of the spaceship, and your police cruiser is complete!

Now it's time to design a police station and jail. Grab a baseplate and construct a building that has an office area and a jail cell.

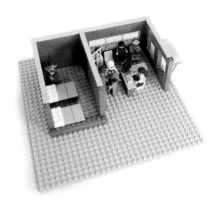

Use a door with bars to separate the office from the jail. You'll want it to be as secure as possible!

Build a workstation with a desk for the police chief, and add chairs to create a waiting area. Make beds for the jail cell. Start with a 4 x 6 brown plate, and add a 1 x 1 brown round plate under each corner for the bed legs. Then add light gray tiles on top, and stack two 2 x 4 white plates to make pillows.

HA! JUST TRY TO CATCH ME!

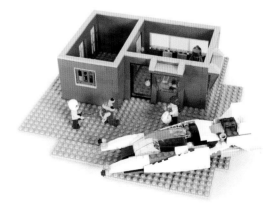

Now it's time for some action! Create a chase scene with an alien and some police officers. Build space rock formations for the alien to attempt to hide behind.

But of course, the alien will be no match for the police force! Off to jail he goes!

SPACESHIP REPAIR DOCK

Jett Griffin is the lead mechanic down at the spaceship repair dock, and he sure knows his stuff. He can tell the difference between a 6.3 mercury converter and a stardust mercury converter in five seconds flat! Jett and his assistant Tony keep all the spaceships in working order. While the mechanics work, pilots can enjoy coffee in the waiting area and chat about the weather . . . which invariably includes discussions about the terrible dust storms on Plexar. Build a tool bench and a shop light for Jett and Tony. Then create a gate that opens and closes to let ships in and out.

PARTS LIST

DARK GRAY BRICKS
1—4 x 10 plate
1—1 x 10 plate
1—1 x 8 plate
4—1 x 6 plates
1—1 x 2 plate
1—2 x 4 plate
2—2 x 2 bricks
16—1 x 2 bricks
1—2 x 3 brick
4—2 x 2 slopes
2—4 x 4 round bricks
1—4 x 4 round plate
2—1 x 2 Technic bricks with two holes

LIGHT GRAY BRICKS
1—4 x 10 plate
1—flexible hose
1—1 x 16 Technic brick
1—1 x 6 Technic brick

1—2 x 6 Technic plate
5—2 x 4 tiles
2—1 x 2 tiles
1—1 x 1 plate with a clip on the side, vertical
4—1 x 1 tiles with a clip on top
1—1 x 2 plate with one clip on top
2—1 x 2—2 x 2 brackets, inverted
1—2 x 2 brick
1—2 x 2 x 3 slope
1—1 x 2 brick
1—1 x 2 x 5 brick

BLACK BRICKS
1—4 x 4 turntable base
1—1 x 1 plate with a clip on the side, vertical
2—2 x 6 plates
4—2 x 2 plates
2—1 x 2 x 2 slopes
8—1 x 2 bricks

4—1 x 2 plates
4—2 x 2 plates with two wheel holders
1—bar, 5 studs long with a handle

ASSORTED BRICKS
1—32 x 32 tan baseplate
4—yellow chairs
8—small wheels
Various tools
1—blue Technic pin, 3 studs long
3—1 x 4 x 2 white bars with studs
1—2 x 2 white round tile with one stud on top
1—2 x 2 white dome
1—2 x 2 translucent yellow round brick
1—2 x 3 x 2 lime green container
2—2 x 4 lime green plates
1—yellow lever (antenna)
1—1 x 1 orange round plate

Build a fuel canister by stacking two 4 x 4 dark gray round bricks on top of a 4 x 4 black turntable base. Place a 2 x 4 dark gray plate on top, as well as two 1 x 1 plates with clips (vertical).

Cover the plates with a 4 x 4 round plate. Now the clips are secure enough to hold a flexible hose in place. Add wheels to the bottom of the canister, and it can be rolled wherever you need it.

Build a shop light. Use a 1 x 2 x 5 light gray brick, a 1 x 2 light gray brick and a 2 x 2 x 3 light gray slope to create a stand for the light. Then find the pieces shown for building the light itself.

Place a 2 x 2 translucent yellow round brick on top of a 2 x 2 white round tile with one stud on top. Then add a 2 x 2 white dome brick.

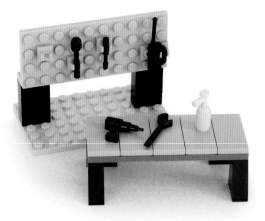

The 1 x 2 x 5 light gray brick that makes up the top of the stand has open studs at the top. Insert a black bar (5 studs long with a handle) into one of the studs. This bar can easily hold the light if you attach a 1 x 1 tile with a clip to the top of the light. The bar will also allow the light to rotate so that you can position it exactly how you want.

Build a workbench! Use 1 x 1 tiles with a clip on top as hooks for hanging tools. The back of the workbench is a 4 x 10 plate. It is attached to two 1 x 2—2 x 2 inverted brackets. The table of the workbench is also a 4 x 10 plate. Cover it with tiles if you have them. Build legs for the table. The back legs are each made up of two 1 x 2 bricks and the front legs are 1 x 2 x 2 slopes.

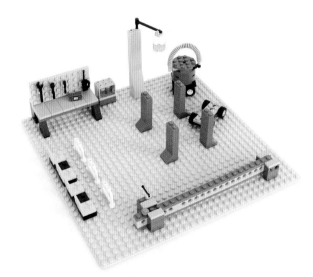

Make a gate for the repair dock that can be raised and lowered. Connect a 1 x 16 Technic brick and a 1 x 6 Technic brick by attaching a row of plates on both the top and the bottom. Insert a blue pin (3 studs long) into the end of the gate. Build two supports that will allow the gate to pivot. Add a 1 x 1 orange round plate on the gate to be a light.

Set up your repair dock on a 32 x 32 baseplate. Attach the gate, and add more supports on the other end. The gate won't connect to these in any way—it will just rest between them. Build benches for the waiting area by placing a 2 x 2 black plate under each end of a 2 x 6 black plate. Make two of these, and then add chairs. Use three 1 x 4 x 2 white bars with studs to separate the waiting area from the repair dock. Build supports for the spaceships.

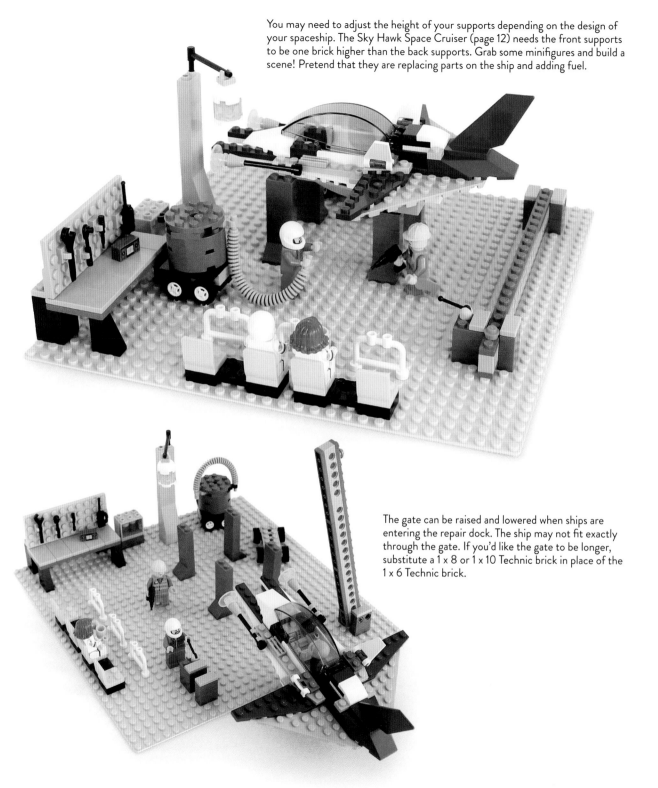

You may need to adjust the height of your supports depending on the design of your spaceship. The Sky Hawk Space Cruiser (page 12) needs the front supports to be one brick higher than the back supports. Grab some minifigures and build a scene! Pretend that they are replacing parts on the ship and adding fuel.

The gate can be raised and lowered when ships are entering the repair dock. The ship may not fit exactly through the gate. If you'd like the gate to be longer, substitute a 1 x 8 or 1 x 10 Technic brick in place of the 1 x 6 Technic brick.

DEEP SPACE RESEARCH CENTER AND ARTICULATED ROVER

"Philip, you left the sliding door open AGAIN," called Greta, slightly annoyed. Hank, Philip and Greta were in charge of studying weather conditions and researching building materials in space. Many people relied on their research to make decisions about space settlements.

"WOW! Look at this!" Hank called. He had discovered a way to combine two metals to create an amazingly strong alloy!

"That's pretty awesome," Greta replied. "I guess I can forgive you for leaving the door open!"

Create a base for exploring deep space and conducting scientific research! This research center has everything, including a mini rocket launch pad, an articulated rover vehicle and a lab full of equipment.

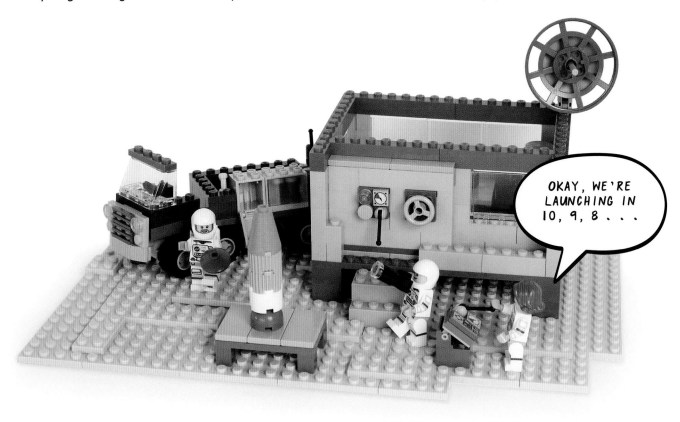

OKAY, WE'RE LAUNCHING IN 10, 9, 8 . . .

PARTS LIST
RESEARCH CENTER BUILDING

ASSORTED BRICKS
2—16 x 16 tan plates
Various tan plates to extend the base (optional)
Various lime green bricks, one stud wide
5—1 x 4 x 3 clear panels
1—1 x 1 translucent light blue round tile
1—1 x 2 lime green plate
2—1 x 1 lime green plates

LIGHT GRAY BRICKS
5—1 x 4 tiles
1—2 x 2 steering wheel
1—lever (antenna)
1—1 x 1 round tile
1—1 x 1 tile with gauges

DARK GRAY BRICKS
1—8 x 16 plate
2—4 x 4 plates
2—2 x 12 plates
1—1 x 8 plate
8—2 x 2 bricks
2—1 x 2—2 x 2 brackets
Various bricks, one stud wide

BUILDING FURNISHINGS
1—4 x 8 dark gray plate
2— 1 x 4 dark gray bricks
4—2 x 4 light gray tiles
2—2 x 3 x 2 light gray containers
1—2 x 6 light gray brick
1—2 x 2 light gray round tile

1—2 x 2 translucent light blue round brick
2—white chairs
2—2 x 2 white plates
1—1 x 2 tile with a computer keyboard
1—1 x 2 tile with a radio
1—1 x 2 medium brown plate
1—1 x 2 hinge brick with a 2 x 2 hinge plate
1—2 x 2 black tile

RADAR
1—6 x 6 dark gray dish (radar)
1—1 x 2 dark gray plate
1—1 x 1 dark gray plate
1—1 x 1 dark gray plate with a clip, horizontal
1—4 x 4 light gray dish
1—light gray bar, 4 studs long
1—1 x 2 dark blue plate
1—1 x 2 light gray plate with handles on both ends
1—1 x 1 black plate with a handle
1—1 x 1 black plate with a clip, horizontal
1—1 x 1 black tile with a clip on top

ROCKET
1—2 x 2 dark gray dome
2—2 x 2 light gray round bricks with ridges
1—2 x 2 white round brick
1—2 x 2 x 2 orange cone

ARTICULATED ROVER

DARK GRAY BRICKS
1—4 x 4 plate
2—1 x 4 plates

2—1 x 3 plates
2—1 x 2 grills
1—6 x 8 plate
1—2 x 6 plate

LIGHT GRAY BRICKS
1—2 x 8 brick
1—2 x 3 brick
1—1 x 2—2 x 2 bracket, inverted
1—1 x 2—1 x 4 bracket
2—1 x 2 plates
1—1 x 2 tile
2—1 x 1 slopes, 30 degree
1—1 x 1 brick with a clip on the side
1—2 x 2 x 2 container
2—1 x 1 plates with a clip, vertical
4—2 x 2 plates with wheel holders
1—2 x 2 plate with a towball socket

DARK BLUE BRICKS
6—1 x 4 bricks
2—1 x 2 bricks
3—1 x 6 plates
1—1 x 1 plate

ASSORTED BRICKS
1—2 x 4 lime green plate
1—2 x 3 x 2 lime green container
1—white steering wheel
1—1 x 2 white plate
1—2 x 4 x 2 windshield
2—1 x 1 translucent yellow round tiles
1—2 x 2 black plate with a towball
8--wheels

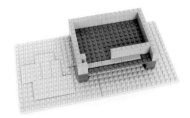

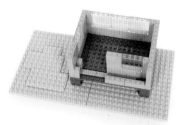

RESEARCH CENTER BUILDING

STEP 1: Two 16 x 16 tan plates make a great foundation for the research center. Create a base for your building. The base in the photo is made out of an 8 x 16 plate, two 2 x 12 plates and a 4 x 4 plate. Use a second 4 x 4 plate underneath these plates to hold them together. Then place two 2 x 2 bricks under each corner of the building. Use three 1 x 4 light gray tiles to build a track for the sliding door.

STEP 2: Build up the walls, and include 1 x 4 x 3 clear panels as windows. If you don't have these, substitute other types of windows. Leave an opening 5 studs wide for the door.

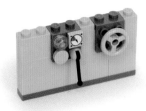

STEP 3: Build the door. Start with a 1 x 8 dark gray plate. Add three rows of lime green bricks, and then attach a 1 x 2—2 x 2 dark gray bracket.

STEP 4: Add a second bracket, and then fill in the row with a 1 x 2 lime green plate and two 1 x 1 lime green plates. Add a steering wheel to one bracket. Decorate the other with buttons and gauges.

STEP 5: Place one more row of lime green bricks on top of the brackets, and then add a row of tiles. This will complete the door.

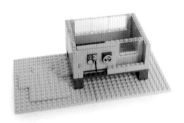

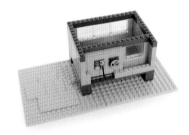

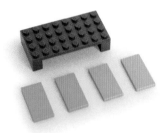

STEP 6: Set the door in place. It does not attach to anything; the bricks in front of the door and behind it will hold it up, and the tiles underneath the door will allow it to slide back and forth.

STEP 7: Finish up the building with a row of dark gray bricks on top.

STEP 8: Use a 4 x 8 plate as a desk for the research center. Place a 1 x 4 dark gray brick under each end. Then cover the desk with four 2 x 4 light gray tiles.

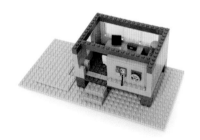

STEP 9: Grab two chairs, and place a 2 x 2 plate under each one. Then build a computer screen by attaching a 2 x 2 black tile to a 1 x 2 hinge brick. Find other accessories, such as a computer keyboard and a radio. Use 2 x 3 x 2 containers to hold supplies. Attach two containers by placing them on top of a 2 x 6 brick.

STEP 10: Place the desk, chairs and cabinets inside the research center. This photo shows the door slid over to its "open" position.

STEP 11: Gather the bricks shown for building a radar unit.

STEP 12: Place a 1 x 1 dark gray plate and a 1 x 1 dark gray plate with a clip (horizontal) on top of a 1 x 2 dark gray plate. Attach a 1 x 1 black plate with a handle to a 1 x 1 black tile with a clip on top. Then add a 1 x 1 black plate with a clip (horizontal).

STEP 13: Use the 1 x 2 light gray plate with handles on both ends to connect the two assemblies from the previous step. Add a 1 x 2 dark blue plate.

STEP 14: Attach the 4 x 4 light gray dish to the 6 x 6 dark gray dish (radar). Insert a bar (4 studs long) in the center of the radar dish. Then attach it to the support as shown.

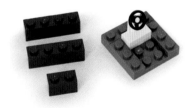

STEP 15: Place the radar assembly on the side of the research center building.

ARTICULATED ROVER
STEP 1: Gather the bricks shown.

STEP 2: Attach a 1 x 4 dark gray plate and two 1 x 3 dark gray plates to a 4 x 4 plate. Add a steering wheel.

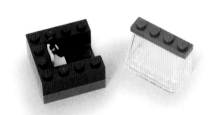

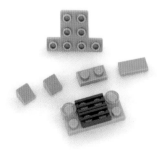

STEP 3: Add two 1 x 4 dark blue bricks and a 1 x 2 dark blue brick. Then find a 2 x 4 x 2 windshield, and place a 1 x 4 dark gray plate on top of it.

STEP 4: Gather the bricks shown for building the front of the vehicle.

STEP 5: Attach the two brackets to each other as shown. Then add two grills and some headlights to the 2 x 4 lime green plate.

STEP 6: Attach the lime green plate to the top bracket. Then place a 1 x 2 light gray plate, a 1 x 2 light gray tile and two 1 x 1 light gray slopes (30 degree) on the lower bracket.

STEP 7: Connect this assembly to the cab of the rover. Then find the bricks shown.

STEP 8: Place the 1 x 2 light gray plate and a 2 x 2 black plate with a towball on top of a 2 x 3 light gray brick.

STEP 9: Attach this to the underside of the cab.

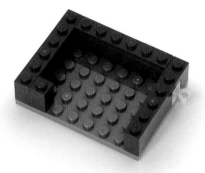

STEP 10: Build the rover's trailer. Grab a 6 x 8 plate and add four 1 x 4 dark blue bricks, a 1 x 2 dark blue brick and a 1 x 1 light gray brick with a clip on the side. Find the dark blue plates shown.

STEP 11: Add a layer of dark blue plates around the perimeter.

STEP 12: Fill in the open space with a 2 x 2 x 2 light gray container and a 2 x 3 x 2 lime green container. These can be used to hold supplies. Grab a 2 x 8 light gray brick, and place a 2 x 6 dark gray plate and a 2 x 2 light gray plate with a towball socket on top of it.

STEP 13: Use the towball and socket to connect the cab and the trailer. Then find four 2 x 2 plates with wheel holders and 8 wheels.

STEP 14: Attach the wheels, and your articulated rover is complete! Articulated means that the cab can turn separately from the trailer. Add tools and other accessories to your rover.

Your astronauts will be able to grab a shovel whenever they need it, and samples of soil and rock can be stored in the containers. Use 1 x 1 round bricks in translucent colors to make bottles. 1 x 1 round tiles make great lids.

Create a scene with your astronauts hard at work! They can launch rockets that will collect important weather data.

Place 1 x 1 translucent orange round bricks under the rocket to make it look like it is blasting off!

ALL-TERRAIN CRANE ROVER

This handy space rover, driven by construction worker Mack Windstorm, is equipped with a clever suspension system. As it rumbles over rocky surfaces, each wheel is free to move up and down independently, which keeps the ride quite stable for the passengers. Equip your rover with a real working crane, or keep the back open for hauling moon rock and other cargo!

PARTS LIST

BLUE BRICKS
1—2 x 6 brick
1—2 x 4 brick
1—1 x 8 brick
3—1 x 6 bricks
8—1 x 4 bricks
1—1 x 8 plate
2—1 x 6 plates
2—1 x 1 bricks
2—1 x 1 bricks with a stud on the side
1—1 x 2 brick
3—2 x 2 slopes
3—2 x 2 inverted slopes
1—1 x 4 brick with 4 studs on the side
4—1 x 7 Technic liftarms
2—3 x 3 wedge plates, cut corners
1—1 x 2 plate

LIGHT GRAY BRICKS
2—6 x 10 plates
1—4 x 10 plate
1—4 x 6 plate
1—1 x 6 plate

1—2 x 4 plate
1—2 x 8 brick
1—1 x 2 plate with two clips on the side
3—2 x 6 bricks
4—2 x 4 bricks
2—1 x 6 bricks
1—2 x 2 brick
2—1 x 8 Technic bricks
1—1 x 6 Technic brick
2—Technic axles, 7 studs long
12—Technic pins
2—1 x 2 grills
1—1 x 3 Technic liftarm with two axle
    holes and a pin/crank
1—bar, 4 studs long
2—wheels with pinholes

DARK GRAY BRICKS
1—4 x 10 plate
2—1 x 14 Technic bricks
2—1 x 15 Technic liftarms
1—2 x 4 brick
1—1 x 4 brick
2—4 x 4 round plates
1—2 x 2 round plate

1—chair
1—6 x 6 dish (radar)

LIME GREEN BRICKS
2—2 x 3 x 2 containers
2—2 x 3 bricks
2—2 x 2 round bricks
1—2 x 2 slope
1—1 x 2 brick

ASSORTED BRICKS
1—3 x 6 x 2 translucent black windshield
2—black Technic pins
1—1 x 2 black plate with a handle on the
    side
1—2 x 2 yellow round plate
2—red Technic bushes
1—red steering wheel
2—1 x 1 translucent orange plates
1—2 x 2 black round tile with ring
8—large wheels with pinholes

OTHER MATERIALS
Thin cotton string

STEP 1: Gather the bricks shown for building the base of the rover vehicle.

STEP 2: Attach the two 1 x 14 Technic bricks to the sides of the 4 x 10 plate. The plate should be centered under the bricks so that the bricks hang off the plate by 2 studs on each side. Then add light gray bricks in the middle.

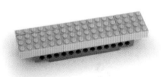

STEP 3: Add another layer of light gray bricks. This layer will also hang off the edge by 2 studs on each end.

STEP 4: The base needs to be just the right height so that the wheels have freedom to move up and down. Add a layer of light gray plates. From left to right, add a 2 x 4 plate, a 4 x 10 plate and a 4 x 6 plate.

STEP 5: Add two 6 x 10 light gray plates. The base should be centered underneath them. However, the plate on the left should line up with the end of the base while the plate on the right hangs off the edge by 2 studs.

STEP 6: Turn the vehicle base over and attach a 4 x 10 dark gray plate on the bottom. Then place three 2 x 2 blue inverted slopes on the front end of the vehicle.

STEP 7: Flip the vehicle base right-side up and add a row of blue bricks around the perimeter. On the front of the vehicle, use a 1 x 4 brick with 4 studs on the side and two 1 x 1 bricks with a stud on the side.

STEP 8: Place a 2 x 4 dark gray brick and a 1 x 4 dark gray brick at the front of the vehicle. Then add a dark gray chair and a steering wheel.

STEP 9: Fill in the front of the vehicle with three 2 x 2 slopes, a 1 x 6 brick and two 1 x 4 bricks.

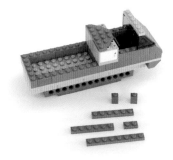

STEP 10: Add a 2 x 4 blue brick and a 1 x 4 blue brick behind the chair. Then find two 2 x 3 x 2 containers and two 2 x 3 lime green bricks.

STEP 11: Attach one container on each side of the vehicle with the two 2 x 3 bricks stacked between them.

STEP 12: Place two 3 x 3 blue wedge plates with cut corners on top of the containers. Then add a 3 x 6 x 2 windshield, and place a 1 x 6 light gray plate along the top of it. Gather the bricks shown.

STEP 13: Attach one 1 x 1 blue brick behind the lime green containers on each side. Then add a row of blue plates around the perimeter of the vehicle.

STEP 14: Gather the bricks shown for building the crane's boom.

STEP 15: Slide the two wheels onto the light gray axle (7 studs long). Then add a liftarm on each side. Keep the liftarms in place by sliding a red Technic bush onto each side of the axle.

STEP 16: Find two 4 x 4 dark gray round plates, two 2 x 2 lime green round bricks, an axle (7 studs long) and a piece of string.

STEP 17: Slide the two round bricks onto the axle. Place the end of the string between the two round bricks, and then attach them to each other. Then add a 4 x 4 dark gray round plate on each side of the axle.

STEP 18: Attach a 1 x 8 light gray Technic brick on each side of the rover and a 1 x 6 light gray Technic brick on the back. Before attaching the Technic bricks to the vehicle, slide the axle for the string assembly through each side of the Technic bricks. Attach the crane's boom by inserting the black pins into the center hole on each light gray Technic brick.

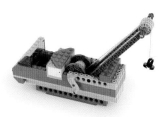

STEP 19: Create a handle to wind the string by attaching a 1 x 3 liftarm (with two axle holes and a pin/crank) to the exposed light gray axle (7 studs long). Tie the end of the string to a 2 x 2 black round tile with a ring. Add a 2 x 6 blue brick to the back of the vehicle to support the crane's boom.

STEP 20: Gather the bricks shown for building a radar device for the rover vehicle.

STEP 21: Build the base for the radar dish as shown. Attach a 2 x 2 dark gray round plate to the radar piece and then insert a light gray bar (4 studs long).

STEP 22: Attach the 2 x 2 yellow round plate to the radar dish and then attach this to the base.

STEP 23: Your rover is almost complete! Attach the radar assembly to the vehicle. Then find two 1 x 2 gray grills and two 1 x 1 translucent orange plates for the front headlights.

STEP 24: Attach the grills and translucent plates as shown.

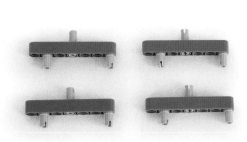

STEP 25: Now it's time to build the suspension system. Find four 1 x 7 liftarms. Insert three light gray pins into each liftarm in the positions shown.

STEP 26: Attach two liftarms to the dark gray Technic bricks on each side of the vehicle. Insert the gray pins into the third hole from the end on the front. Use the second hole from the end on the back.

STEP 27: Attach a large wheel to each of the eight pins. Your crane rover is complete!

Now it's time for some planet exploration! If the rover encounters rough terrain, the wheels will move up and down over the bumps one at a time while the body of the vehicle maintains a smooth ride.

If you don't have the pieces needed for the crane, you can easily make your rover into a rock hauler! Simply leave the bed of the vehicle open.

Then your space guys can excavate rock and load it into the rover!

EXCAVATING DRILL MECH

Marshall Grady enjoys waking up early and putting in a solid day's work on the construction site. His Excavating Drill Mech combines heavy-duty excavating capabilities with robotic technology. From up in the cab, he can operate the arms, and the body can rotate from side to side. It's perfect for drilling to find valuable ore or for building new space settlements!

PARTS LIST

DARK GRAY BRICKS
1—2 x 12 plate
1—4 x 4 round brick
1—4 x 4 round brick with four side pinholes
1—4 x 4 round plate
1—1 x 2 Technic brick with two holes
1—1 x 2 plate
2—1 x 1 round plates
1—1 x 4 x 1 panel
2—Technic axle and pin connectors #1
1—Technic axle and pin connector #4
1—bar with a clip

LIGHT GRAY BRICKS
2—2 x 3 x 2 containers
2—2 x 4 plates with two pins
1—2 x 4 plate
2—1 x 2 plates

1—1 x 2 plate with two clips on the side
2—Technic axles, 3 studs long
1—Technic axle and pin connector #5
2—1 x 2 x 1⅓ bricks modified with a curved top
1—Technic bush
1—1 x 4 plate modified with angled tubes
2—1 x 1 tiles with gauges
1—1 x 2 tile with gauges
1—drill (LEGO ID 64713)

BLACK BRICKS
1—Technic axle, 8 studs long
1—2 x 8 plate
1—4 x 4 turntable base, locking
2—1 x 2 bricks with ridges
1—Technic axle connector 2L, smooth
2—Technic pins with friction ridges
1—6 x 4 x 3⅓ windshield roll cage

BLUE BRICKS
1—1 x 2 tile
1—1 x 4 tile
2—1 x 4 plates
3—1 x 2 bricks
2—Technic pins, ½ length

RED BRICKS
3—Technic bushes
1—Technic axle, 2 studs long with notches
2—1 x 1 bricks with a stud on the side (headlight)
1—2 x 2 turntable

ASSORTED BRICKS
4—large wheels with pinholes
2—10 x 2 x 2 yellow slopes, double
2—2 x 2 translucent neon green round bricks
2—yellow levers (antennas)
1—4 x 6 yellow plate

STEP 1: Grab a 2 x 12 dark gray plate, a 2 x 8 black plate and two 2 x 4 light gray plates with two pins.

STEP 2: Attach the black plate and the two light gray plates to the 2 x 12 dark gray plate.

STEP 3: Add two 2 x 2 translucent neon green round bricks and two 1 x 2 black bricks with ridges. If you don't have the bricks with ridges, substitute any 1 x 2 bricks.

STEP 4: Place two 10 x 2 x 2 yellow slope bricks on the base of the drill mech. Then find a 1 x 4 light gray plate modified with angled tubes, a 1 x 2 light gray plate, a 4 x 4 black turntable base and a 1 x 4 blue tile.

STEP 5: Place these bricks on top of the yellow slope bricks as shown. The 1 x 2 light gray plate goes under the 1 x 4 light gray plate with tubes.

STEP 6: Attach a 4 x 4 dark gray round brick and a 4 x 4 dark gray round plate to the turntable base. Then find the bricks shown.

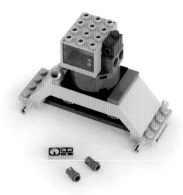

STEP 7: Place the two light gray containers on the 4 x 4 round plate. Then add the 1 x 2 Technic brick with two holes and the two 1 x 1 red bricks with a stud on the side.

STEP 8: Insert the two blue pins into the holes on the Technic brick, and then use the pins to attach a 1 x 2 tile with gauges to the machine.

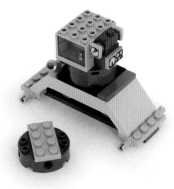

STEP 9: Find a 4 x 4 round brick with pinholes in the sides. The holes will be used to hold the robotic arms. Then find the other bricks shown.

STEP 10: Attach the 2 x 4 light gray plate on top of the 4 x 4 round brick. Then place a 1 x 1 dark gray round plate and a 1 x 1 tile with a gauge on each 1 x 1 red brick.

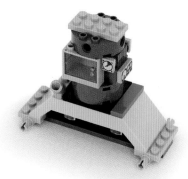

STEP 11: Attach the 4 x 4 round brick and the 2 x 4 plate to the top of the containers.

STEP 12: Center a 4 x 6 yellow plate on top of the drill mech. Then find the bricks shown.

STEP 13: Stack two 1 x 4 blue plates at the front of the mech. Then add three 1 x 2 blue bricks on the second row of studs from the back as shown. Add a 1 x 2 light gray plate with two clips on the side so that the clips face the back.

STEP 14: Add a 1 x 2 light gray plate on top of the 1 x 2 blue bricks, and then attach two 1 x 2 x 1⅓ bricks modified with a curved top and a 1 x 2 blue tile on top of that. Place a 1 x 4 x 1 dark gray panel at the front of the drill mech. Find the bricks shown.

STEP 15: Attach a black 6 x 4 x 3⅓ windshield roll cage to the clips on the back of the cab. Place a 2 x 2 turntable on top of the cab, and attach a 1 x 2 dark gray plate and two yellow levers (antennas) just behind the blue plates at the front of the cab.

STEP 16: Gather the bricks shown for building the first robotic arm.

STEP 17: Insert a black pin and a red axle (2 studs long with notches) into a dark gray Technic connector #1.

STEP 18: Slide a light gray Technic connector #5 onto the red axle. Then insert a light gray axle (3 studs long).

STEP 19: Add a red Technic bush and a black axle connector 2L (1 x 2 smooth). Slide a bar with a clip (looks like a wrench) into the black connector.

STEP 20: Gather the bricks shown for building the second arm.

STEP 21: Insert a black pin and a light gray axle (3 studs long) into a Technic connector #1.

STEP 22: Slide a light gray Technic bush onto the axle. Then add a dark gray Technic connector #4.

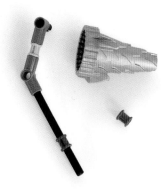

STEP 23: Insert a black axle (8 studs long) and then slide a red Technic bush about a third of the way up the axle.

STEP 24: Slide the drill onto the axle, and slide another red Technic bush onto the axle to keep the drill from coming off.

STEP 25: Insert both arms into the holes in the 4 x 4 round brick underneath the cab. Then find four large wheels with pinholes.

STEP 26: Attach the wheels, and the drill mech is complete! The turntable allows it to rotate from side to side. Find a driver to operate the controls. The black pins in the arms have friction ridges, so the arms will stay put at whatever height you pose them.

Try building a mountain out of bricks, and pretend that your drill is powering through solid rock. Loose bricks around the bottom make it look like rock is falling as the drill does its job!

Then create a scene with the Excavating Drill Mech and the All-Terrain Crane Rover (page 136) working together to excavate a rock mountain!

HOVERING SHUTTLE SERVICE

Skip Houston can transport passengers all around Plexar in his hovering shuttle service! Build multiple cars and attach them with ball and socket joints. Then construct a station with benches so that passengers can wait for their ride on the hovering shuttle. All passengers must be seated with their hands inside the vehicle before taking off! Have a safe trip!

PARTS LIST

LIGHT GRAY BRICKS
2—4 x 8 plates
1—2 x 8 plate
2—1 x 7 liftarms
2—1 x 2 x 1 panels
2—1 x 2 plates with handles
2—1 x 2 plates with a socket on the side
1—1 x 1 tile with a gauge

DARK GRAY BRICKS
1—1 x 4 Technic brick
4—2 x 4 plates
2—1 x 4 plates
4—1 x 2 plates
1—2 x 2 round plate
1—1 x 2—1 x 2 bracket, inverted
2—1 x 2 plates with a ball on the side

BLUE BRICKS
4—1 x 6 bricks
2—1 x 4 bricks
2—1 x 2 bricks
4—1 x 1 bricks
1—3 x 6 wedge plate
1—2 x 3 slope

3—1 x 4 plates
2—1 x 1 plates
2—1 x 1 bricks with a stud on the side
4—1 x 1 slopes, 30 degree
2—Technic pins with friction ridges, 3 studs long

WHITE BRICKS
1—3 x 6 wedge plate, right
1—3 x 6 wedge plate, left
1—2 x 6 plate
1—1 x 2 plate with a handle on the side, free ends

YELLOW BRICKS
1—steering wheel
4—chairs
1—lever (antenna)
1—1 x 2 plate
2—1 x 1 translucent yellow round tiles
2—2 x 2 translucent yellow dishes
1—1 x 2 tile with a handle

ASSORTED BRICKS
2—1 x 1 translucent red round plates
4—2 x 2 black round plates with a rounded bottom

STATION

LIGHT GRAY BRICKS
1—6 x 14 plate
1—6 x 10 plate
1—4 x 10 plate
1—4 x 4 plate

ASSORTED BRICKS
12—1 x 2 blue bricks
4—2 x 4 dark blue slopes
2—2 x 2 dark blue slopes
4—2 x 2 dark blue double convex slopes
1—green trash can
4—2 x 6 lime green plates
4—1 x 2 lime green bricks
4—1 x 2 dark gray hinge plates with one finger
4—1 x 2 dark gray hinge plates with two fingers
1—1 x 8 x 2 dark gray bar

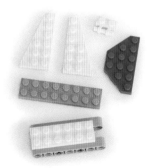

STEP 1: Find two 1 x 7 light gray liftarms and a 1 x 4 dark gray Technic brick. Then find two blue pins with frictions ridges (3 studs long).

STEP 2: Insert the pins through the holes on both ends of the Technic brick as shown.

STEP 3: Slide the two 1 x 7 liftarms onto the blue pins.

STEP 4: Attach a 2 x 6 white plate to the studs on the top of the Technic brick. Then find the bricks shown.

STEP 5: Place two 3 x 6 white wedge plates and a 3 x 6 blue wedge plate on top of the shuttle.

STEP 6: Then add a 2 x 8 light gray plate and a 1 x 2 white plate with a handle on the side (free ends).

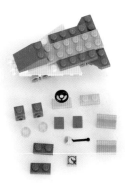

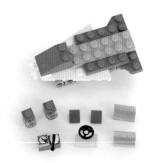

STEP 7: Place a 1 x 4 blue plate on each side of the shuttle and then add a 2 x 3 slope at the front. Then gather the bricks shown.

STEP 8: Make two headlights by attaching translucent yellow round tiles to 1 x 1 blue bricks with a stud on the side. Then attach a 1 x 1 tile with a gauge and a lever (antenna) to a 1 x 2 dark gray plate.

STEP 9: Place the headlights and the cockpit controls on the shuttle. Then add a steering wheel.

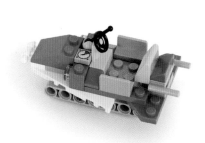

STEP 10: Attach a 1 x 2 x 1 light gray panel on each side of the cockpit. Place a 1 x 1 blue slope on each side of the steering wheel. Then find the bricks shown.

STEP 11: Place a 2 x 2 dark gray round plate on the back of the shuttle. Then add a 1 x 2 yellow tile with a handle and a 1 x 2 light gray plate with handles behind that. Attach two 1 x 1 blue slopes to the light gray plate with handles.

STEP 12: Find a 1 x 4 blue plate, two 1 x 1 blue plates, a 1 x 4 dark gray plate and a 1 x 2 light gray plate with a socket on the side.

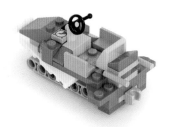

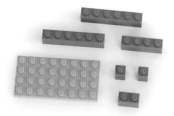

STEP 13: Stack the plates as shown. This assembly will allow the cockpit of the shuttle to attach to a car behind it.

STEP 14: Attach the socket assembly to the back of the shuttle.

STEP 15: Gather the bricks shown for building the end car for the shuttle.

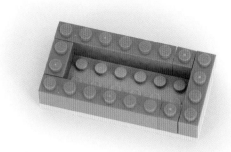

STEP 16: Build a row of blue bricks around the perimeter of a light gray 4 x 8 plate.

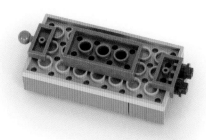

STEP 17: Turn the shuttle car over and add a 1 x 2 plate with a ball on the side, two 2 x 4 dark gray plates and a 1 x 2—1 x 2 dark gray bracket, inverted. Add two 1 x 1 translucent red round plates to be tail lights.

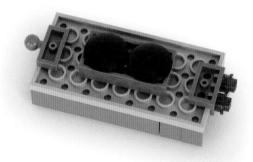

STEP 18: Add two 2 x 2 black round plates with a rounded bottom.

STEP 19: Repeat steps 15 through 18 to make as many middle cars as you'd like! The only difference is that the middle cars will need to have a ball on the front end and a socket on the back end.

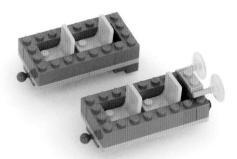

STEP 20: Add chairs where your passengers will sit. Then attach a 1 x 2 light gray plate with handles to the end car. Slide a 2 x 2 translucent neon yellow dish onto each handle.

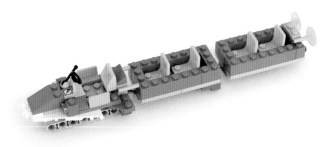

STEP 21: Once you have all of your cars built, you're ready to assemble your shuttle. Insert each towball into a socket to connect the cars. Your shuttle is complete!

Try building a station for your hovering shuttle service. Passengers can sit on the benches while they wait.

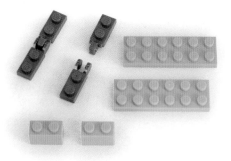

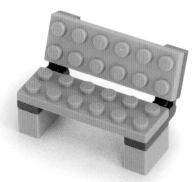

Assembling the benches is quite easy. Gather the bricks shown to build a bench.

Attach two 2 x 6 lime green plates to two sets of hinge plates. Then use 1 x 2 lime green bricks for the legs.

Load up your hovering shuttle with passengers, and send them off on a journey! Maybe they are traveling to watch the alien speeder races (page 88).

ZOOMING JET PACKS

Send your minifigures on a space quest with their own personal jet packs on their backs! It's fun to skip the spaceship and simply zoom through space! Construct a couple of different styles of jet packs, and then you'll definitely want to try building a personal hovercraft as well.

PARTS LIST

YELLOW BRICKS
1—2 x 2 yellow dome
1—2 x 2 yellow round brick
1—1 x 2 yellow Technic brick
1—1 x 2 yellow plate

ASSORTED BRICKS
2—1 x 2 light gray plates with handles on both ends
1—1 x 2—2 x 2 light gray bracket, inverted
1—blue Technic axle pin
2—1 x 1 dark gray cones

2—2 x 2 white flags
2—flames
1—clear minifigure neck bracket with 2 studs

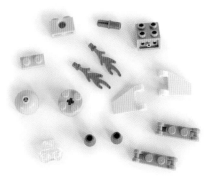

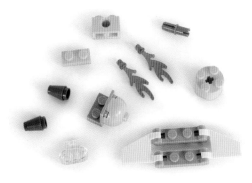

Build a jet pack that attaches to a neck bracket on a minifigure. The neck bracket provides 2 studs to attach things to. Gather the bricks shown.

Use two 1 x 2 light gray plates with handles on both ends to attach two 2 x 2 white flags. Then attach a 2 x 2 yellow dome brick to a 1 x 2—2 x 2 bracket (inverted).

Attach the bracket to the upper light gray plate between the white flags. Place a 1 x 2 yellow plate on top of a 1 x 2 yellow Technic brick.

Connect the yellow Technic brick and plate to the light gray bracket. Then insert a blue axle pin into the hole on the Technic brick.

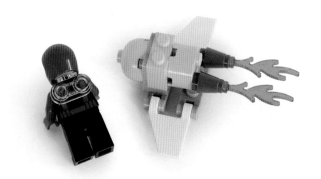

Slide the 2 x 2 yellow round brick onto the blue axle with the studs facing down. Then attach two 1 x 1 dark gray cones and insert a flame into each cone.

Put a clear neck bracket on a minifigure by removing the head, sliding the bracket over the neck and then putting the head back on. Now you're ready to attach the jet pack!

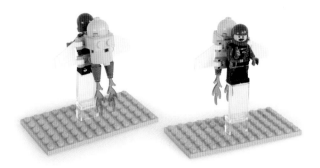

Use clear bricks and panels to prop up your minifigures and to create scenes where they are blasting off to space!

Another way to create a jet pack is to use 1 x 2 plates with a handle on the side. Minifigures can hold onto the handles. Use brackets to attach details, such as tiles with buttons and controls.

Use 1 x 1 cones or round bricks to create rocket engines, and a lever (antenna) looks great on top of the jet pack!

Light gray Technic pins, ½ length with 2-stud-long bar extension (flick missiles), are perfect for attaching flames to the bottom of a jet pack. Use 1 x 1 plates with a clip (vertical) to hold the pins.

Another fun idea for personal space travel is to build a hovercraft.

The base of this hovercraft is a 6 x 6 light gray round plate. Add panels on the sides and build some cockpit controls. Small 2 x 3 wedge plates make tiny wings on the sides. Build the hovering base with a 6 x 6 dish (radar). The dish will attach to the bottom of the hovercraft with the curved side up.

ACKNOWLEDGMENTS

I am so thankful for everyone who contributed their skill and creativity to this book!

Thank you Page Street Publishing and especially my editor, Sarah. Your ideas and encouragement helped me make this book the best it could be! I could not have done it without you.

I am so extremely grateful for the following 10- to 15-year-old boys who contributed project ideas to this book. You all are fantastic spaceship inventors!

Thank you to Peter Wyatt for creating the design for the Gravity Force Spinning Space Shuttles. This is such an excellent project to build!

Thank you to Baxter Connell for designing the Z-3 Explorer spaceship. This ship is one of our favorites!

Thank you to Noah Zachary for designing the Yellow Hornet Fighter Ship. It's an awesome ship!

Thank you to Aiden Barnes for designing the Flight Simulator and the Excavating Drill Mech. I so appreciate you building these creative and fun projects!

Thank you to my son Owen Dees for designing the Sky Hawk Space Cruiser, the Intergalactic Transporter, some of the mini ships, the Rocket Launch Pad, the Spaceship Repair Dock, the Police Cruiser Spaceship, one of the alien speeders, one of the flying saucers and the Turbo Booster Alien Ship.

Thank you to my son Gresham Dees for designing the Canine Cruiser 4.0, one of the alien speeders, the Epic Battle Tank and the Astro-Bots.

Thank you to my son Aidan Dees for designing the Weightlessness Training project. I knew you could make that happen!

Most of all, I am so thankful for my husband, Jordan, and his unending support for all my creative pursuits! Thank you for putting up with LEGO bricks everywhere and constant discussions about what we should build next. Our life is such a fun adventure!

ABOUT THE AUTHOR

Sarah Dees is the creative mind behind the popular website Frugal Fun for Boys and Girls. She's the author of three other LEGO project books: *Awesome LEGO® Creations with Bricks You Already Have, Epic LEGO® Adventures with Bricks You Already Have* and *Genius LEGO® Inventions with Bricks You Already Have.* She is an educator; wife to her wonderful husband, Jordan; and a busy mom of five LEGO-loving kids. She enjoys learning and exploring the outdoors with her kids, as well as creating all kinds of neat LEGO projects. It's not unusual for her playroom floor to be covered with LEGO bricks—with the entire family building! Her website is a fantastic resource for crafts, activities, STEM projects and games that kids will love. Check out her latest projects, including LEGO ideas, at frugalfun4boys.com.

INDEX